Cheyenne Journey

Cheyenne Journey
Morning Star, Our Guiding Light

The Dull Knife Memorial Foundation
Learning From the Wisdom of the Past for Tomorrow

by Doreen "Walking Woman" Pond and Arthur L. McDonald

Foreword by
Senator Ben Nighthorse Campbell

SEVEN LOCKS PRESS
Santa Ana, California
Minneapolis, Minnesota
Washington, D.C.

Printed in Hong Kong

Library of Congress Cataloging-in-Publication Data

Pond, Doreen, 1946–
    Cheyenne Journey: Morning Star, Our Guiding Light / by Doreen "Walking Woman" Pond and Arthur L. McDonald
        p. 160 cm.
    "The Dull Knife Memorial Foundation: Learning from the Wisdom of the Past for Tomorrow."
    ISBN 0-929765-50-8
    1. Cheyenne Indians--History.   2. Northern Cheyenne Indian Reservation (Mont.)
3. Cheyenne Indians--Pictorial works.
I. McDonald, Arthur L.   II. Dull Knife Memorial Foundation   III. Title.

    E99.C53P55   1996
978.6'32--dc21   96-36980
                                         CIP

Page xii	Photo by Glenn Asakawa courtesy of *Rocky Mountain News*
Pages xvi, 29, 34, 43 & 45	Photos courtesy of St. Labre Indian School
Pages xviii & 111	Illustration ©Douglas Buchman, The Big Pixel
Page 5	Photo by Larry Mayer courtesy of *The Billings Gazette*
Pages 11 & 39	Photos courtesy of D. Linthacum
Page 37	Photo by Michael Crummett
Page 59	Photo courtesy of L. A. Huffman

The authors will not receive any remuneration from the sales or commissions of this book. All proceeds will go to the Dull Knife Memorial Foundation.

SEVEN LOCKS PRESS
P.O. Box 25689
Santa Ana, CA 92799
(800) 354-5348

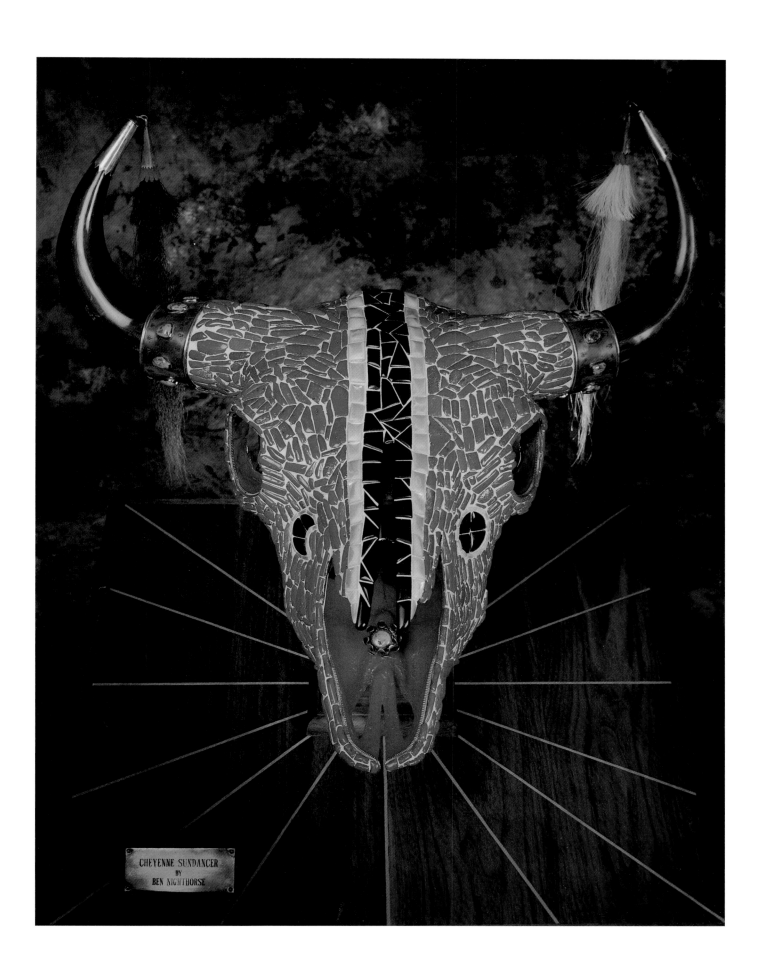

CHEYENNE SUNDANCER
BY
BEN NIGHTHORSE

This symbol is the Morning Star, the official emblem of the Northern Cheyenne tribe. It represents the sacred wisdom of the past and the power that will guide us all into the future.

Morning Star, *Wohehiv*, was the name given to Chief Dull Knife, who led our people over 100 years ago to our home in Montana today. Wohehiv helped see us through the winter of our lives, and in the early years, in the fall of our people, as the morning light rising in the East begins a new day, so the Morning Star inspired, guided, and united us as a tribe in the spirit of hope.

It is a hope not only for the Northern Cheyenne people but for all of America, and for the world, as we struggle together to survive.

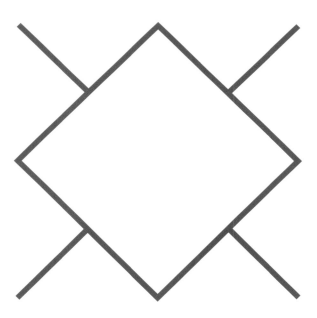

Table of Contents

Foreword

*S*enator Ben Nighthorse Campbell.

It is a great privilege and honor for me to write the foreword to *Cheyenne Journey*. This book is a very interesting and unique way of presenting the wisdom of the Cheyenne elders to a new generation of listeners.

A few years ago during a very trying period of my life, I returned to the source of my ancestry searching for direction and for an understanding of the perplexing experiences of life. The Cheyenne elders were like a gift of light for me. They were willing to listen, and they truly understood the important difference between "acceptance" vs. "approval."

They accepted me for what I was, and part of that acceptance was a commitment to share their wisdom with me. They did not push or force me into paying allegiance to their particular viewpoints, but rather offered it for my acceptance. I began to see that value can exist in other than material, tangible items. I could now appreciate the value of traditions, and it was through the storytelling of the elders that it all started coming together for me.

The Cheyenne have much to share with all of America, about how to live, how to take care of the land and each other, and how to begin anew amidst the problems we face as a people and as a nation. Perhaps *Cheyenne Journey* will be a way for many to understand the wisdom of the elders, and the Morning Star will be the Guiding Light to lead the way.

Ben Nighthorse Campbell
U.S. Senator, Colorado
Member, Northern Cheyenne

Acknowledgments

Nothing as complex as this endeavor is ever accomplished without a great deal of effort on the part of many. We want to recognize each and every contribution to this work, but that is impossible. Therefore, we will hit only the high spots. First, the crew from California: Paul Glass, Jim Riordan, and Dan "Pickle" Schaeffer from Seven Locks Press, Heather Slade of Sparrow Advertising & Design, and Roberta Shepherd, editor. Their 18-hour workdays interrupted only by their constant "nagging" of the Reservation crew kept the project moving.

Thanks go to Fr. Emmett Hoffmann for his encouragement, patience, great ideas, and his willingness to help with the tedious tasks. And to John Warner whose artistry is evident in the photography.

As always, without the belief and support of our families, nothing of any importance would have taken place.

A special thanks to Senator Ben Nighthorse Campbell. He has supported the Foundation in so many ways since the very beginning including the donation of the art masterpiece, *Cheyenne Sundancer*, and the creation of the *Cheyenne Sunrise*, a special buckle used to raise money for the development of an art curriculum at the College.

This book doesn't really belong to the authors. It is a brief summary of the lessons we have been privileged to learn from our elders, the heroes of our generation—John Woodenlegs, Allen Rowland, Bernadine Fisher—who shared their wisdom with us before passing on; and especially Bill Tallbull and Ted Risingsun who gave us guidance and encouragement in the creation of the College and the Foundation, and who are quoted throughout the book. The process is continuing with new lessons from Rose Medicine Elk, Dorothy Flatness, Helen Hiwalker, and Lucille Spear.

Special recognition is due to the Foundation board members and contemporary leaders in our community: Norma Bixby, Rubie Sooktis, Windy Soulderblade, and Tony Foote as well as Freida Standingelk who, with their wisdom, foresight, and dedication, made Dull Knife Memorial College and the Dull Knife Memorial Foundation possible.

Thanks are due for the poetry of Leland "Jim" Pond Jr., and for the special poem at the beginning of the summer session from a special little girl who was a shining light for all of us, MartyAnna McDonald.

A very special thank you from the junior author to my 93-year-old father, Justin McDonald, who for the past 61 years has provided me with standards of principles, values, and behavioral conduct that I am still trying to reach. I can only hope that my legacy will be as rich.

Introduction

Americans have a heritage of survival. Adversity has only made us stronger. Historically, we have always faced the uncertain future with a faith in ourselves to meet any challenge. Yet, as we approach the new millennium, we are experiencing a sense of powerlessness, an uneasy feeling that we are at a crossroads and have lost our way.

The causes of our distress are many: an uncertain economy, a decline in traditional institutions—broken families, rising divorce rate, pervasive crime—a growing ecological crisis, and a technological transformation to the Information Age.

Underlying these symptoms of distress are a crisis of values and a loss of direction and purpose. Yet, there is a source of inspiration we can draw upon, a wellspring of knowledge and experience to guide us on the unfamiliar paths ahead: the wisdom of the American Indians who have themselves survived and flourished despite the many ways in which we have undermined their traditional culture. They contain within their tribal communities the seeds of wisdom that have kept their peoples together, often with notable success.

American Indian history is one of change, whether self-imposed or thrust upon them. In all circumstances they have met each challenge with courage, drawing upon their strong sense of values, their recognition of the importance of the tribe, and their love of the land which sustains them.

A shining example is the success of the Northern Cheyenne Morning Star people in their efforts to create a college and a foundation for the purpose of preserving their culture and educating their people. Located on the reservation at Lame Deer, Montana, the Dull Knife Memorial College, with one of the lowest drop-out rates in the country, is educating students in the traditional ways while preparing them for the technological future.

We need the wisdom of the American Indians to grow as individuals, as a community, as a nation, and as a human species.

The Northern Cheyenne elders have agreed it is time to speak out, to share their wisdom of the ages. They do this for themselves, for the planet as a whole, for this generation, and for the generations to come.

Cheyenne Journey offers this message.

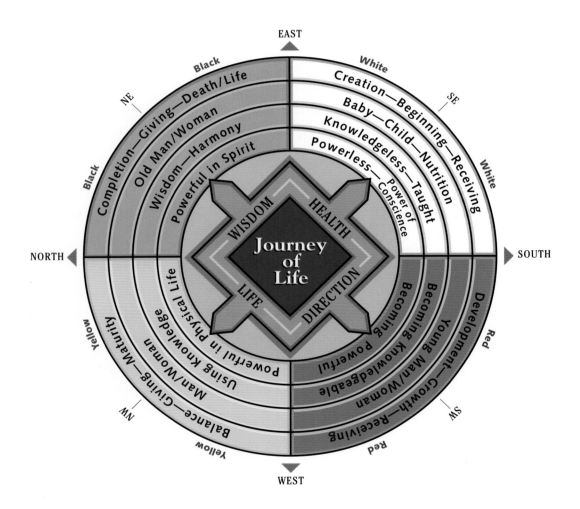

This spiral represents the cycle of life from birth through adolescence to maturity, and finally into the age of wisdom. Each stage has its own cycle of learning, reaching toward completion. The Journey of Life symbol was developed by Lucille Spear and Flora Red Robe Seminole.

The Seasons

The seasons have always been a central part of our life. When we were hunters and gatherers, there were the seasons of the game as we traveled from place to place searching for food. And year after year, the seasons—fall, winter, spring, and summer— would repeat themselves until it was fall again.

When we became farmers we followed the seasons

from harvest

to the barrenness of winter

to the renewal of spring

to the joy and fulfillment of summer.

In American Indian tradition seasons are linked to the four cardinal directions, beginning with the East where the morning star rises. Each direction has its own color: East, white; South, red; West, yellow; and North, black.

All things travel in a circle. Thus, as the seasons form a circle in time from year to year, so do the directions as we turn around in one place. The sun, too, moves around the earth from East to West, returning to the East to rise again. This is the Journey of Life.

The seasons of the human being developed from these concepts.

East is the beginning. This is spring, the creation or birth, and is represented by the color white for purity.

South is the summer of the child who, upon reaching adolescence, is educated with the proper teaching. This is represented by red which stands for growth.

West and Fall bring maturity. The adult who follows the right path achieves respect and honor, represented by yellow for fulfillment.

North is the time of winter when the adult becomes one of the elders, when knowledge leads to wisdom. It is a state of completion represented by the color black.

The circle of life is complete and one returns to the Creator to begin anew.

Leaves

A leaf falls
Helplessly from a tree
The wind calls
Beckoning the spirit within me.

The wind carries the golden knight
From highs to lows
Such as a life carries all within sight
From the summer sound, to the silence of the
snows
The invisible walls
Rise as time runs rampant and free
Each one to be overcome
And conquered by you and me.

Each time the fright
Increases and grows
So will the light
As the wind whispers and blows.

Fall is the beginning of the Cheyenne seasonal year, therefore our early history is the beginning of our seasons. It is a time of harvest when the fruits of the last season are reaped.

Before the coming of the white man, our early history was told through tales and legends. Even after our people passed into written history with the arrival of the Europeans in the 1600s, the elders told these stories to the tribe, and tribal members passed them on to our children. Some of the stories were very ancient tales of the earliest Cheyenne ancestors. Others were contemporary and told of the white traders and settlers who began arriving in the mid-1600s. But they were told in our way.

The past lives on in the present. We can draw upon the stories of our history to sustain and strengthen us today. For that is the source of the wisdom we bring to the future. It is our guide to tomorrow.

Tribal Legend
My people gathered on the shores of a mighty river and
began crossing the ice in search of new lands.
My lovely maiden had crossed, and I would cross later.
Before I could cross, the ice began to crack and churn.
We could not cross this mighty river.
We returned to the crossing many times but never saw
our people again.
With a tortured soul and a tireless body I searched
the generations for my maiden.
When you held my hand
The turmoil in my soul began to subside.
My aching body began to ease.
Is my search over? With hope I ask,
Are you my maiden?
If the answer is yes,
It is a beautiful way to end a legend.
                              Bill Tallbull, 1989

Only known photograph of Bill Tallbull, taken from newspaper archives.

Cheyenne legends

Myths, legends, rituals, and ceremonies have always been an integral part of Cheyenne Indian life. The stories were, and are, our way of passing along the traditional wisdom of our people and of explaining how things important to our people were created. Each person tells these stories differently, but the core truth or message remains.

Bill Tallbull, elder, advisor, and former professor of history at the Dull Knife Memorial College, has left behind an abundant legacy of Cheyenne Indian legends. One of these is the creation story of the Cheyenne Tsistsistas, "beautiful people."

In the beginning there was a large body of water. There was no land anywhere. A person was floating on the water. Water birds swam beside him. They talked among themselves, saying, "We get tired swimming and living in the water. Let's go ask this person if there's something he can do. He must be tired floating on the water himself."

So they went to him saying, "We'd like to get out of this water, but there's no land anywhere." He answered, "The only land is at the bottom of this lake. Someone is going to have to go down and get a piece of land for I cannot."

So the birds dove down to pick up some mud from the bottom, but they couldn't reach down that far. Then the little mud duck said, "I'd like to try." They laughed at him, thinking that this little bird couldn't possibly do what they could not. Nevertheless, the little mud duck went down and brought up the mud. He gave it to the person who took it and rolled it in his hand to make a ball. He kept rolling it until it dried and became dust. As the birds waited in suspense, the person merely blew the dust upon the waters and the land appeared. It grew and grew. The ducks said, "We've been swimming all this time, and now we have a place to walk."

So the Earth appeared.

Then this person took a piece of the Earth and formed a person which was man. Then after a time, a woman. This was the beginning of the Earth and Man.

Now that we are part of history, historians have given us our own place in that flow. According to anthropologists and linguists, we are part of the Algonquin-speaking peoples who settled in the area that became the Northern United States and Southern Canada, extending from the Rocky Mountains to the shores of the Atlantic.

For a long time (perhaps 10,000 years ago) the Cheyennes lived along the shores of the Great Lakes region in territory that is now Minnesota. About 1000-2000 years ago

(although no one knows exactly) our people began the first of many migrations. We left the lakes and moved southward in dugout canoes to what is now Northern Minnesota. It was in the mid-1600s at this settlement that the dog first became a part of camp life.

At first the dogs were wild and very much like wolves in size, although different in color. As we gave them food they became more friendly and eventually tame. In time, people began using them to carry things as we moved from place to place.

There was a time when the Great Spirit talked to the animals about becoming friends with a two-legged person. "Which of you would like to become the partner of this two-legged?" The animals declined. No one wanted to be friends with this two-legged.

A dog said, "I'd like to be the one," but he hesitated. The Great Spirit said, "Would you be a friend if I give you something I have not given the other animals?" The dog asked, "What is it?"

"There are two things I'm going to give you to help you serve this person," the Great Spirit said. "First, the ability to see in the dark. You will be the only one to see danger coming in the night. And in time of famine all you have to do is wish for meat. In this way the person will eat and then you, in turn, will eat."

"What is the second thing you're going to give me?" the dog wanted to know. The Great Spirit answered, "When your person goes to the Happy Hunting Ground, you will go with him." So the dog said, "Then I will be the animal that will help this person."

Dogs began to carry on their backs the small hunting lodges and tepees made of poles covered by sheets of bark or reed mats. They carried the travois, a wooden sled made of two trailing poles with a platform for the load. Legend has it that the dog's special gift of seeing at night helped create great warriors too.

In those days when people traveled on foot, they moved their camp in the summer to the mountains. Along the way, men hunted and women and children gathered berries. Each evening they all returned to camp to share their food with the group.

There are many legends about journeying. They are parables with a message to teach. This is one of them.

One day when the women were scattered about the foothills gathering berries, one of them suddenly began screaming. Others came running to see a bear grab a woman and take her away. The women stood by helplessly, afraid. But the bear did not harm the woman. He took her to the mountains where he put her inside a cave, rolling a stone over the entrance.

Inside the cave was a bear cub. In time, the woman became like a mother to him. The cub grew and grew and one day as he was playing, he said, "Mother, why do you cry all the time?" "I am lonesome for my people. Even if I could get out of here, I wouldn't know where to find them."

When the cub was older he said, "Mother, one day soon we will leave this cave." She asked, "How are we going to move the stone?" The cub said, "I can move it. Make extra moccasins as we will have a long way to go."

More time went by. Then one day when the bear left the cave to seek food, the cub said, "Today is the day." He rolled the stone out of the way, and the woman and the cub ran and ran. Sometimes the mother picked up the cub and carried him. Sometimes she took him by the hand and they ran together. When she thought she couldn't go on, the cub would say, "Change your moccasins." When she did, she was no longer tired.

They stopped to rest and the mother said, "You must know where we're going. I don't." The cub said, "I know where your people are. We must swim across the river several times so the bear can't track us."

After running for days and days the cub said, "We are coming to the camp of your people." When they arrived, the cub was on her back, and he said, "Let me walk and you hold my hand."

There was much rejoicing in the camp over the woman's return. And after that the cub lived with his mother and her people as he was, becoming one of the little boys in the camp.

Bear Cub and two other boys in the camp went on a long journey in which they discovered new things about the land. Many of our traditions are derived from this journey and are still celebrated today.

In the camp Bear Cub played with the other boys who became his friends. One was named Fast Runner because when antelope came to drink, Fast Runner would chase and catch them, and there would be meat to eat.

Another one of the boys was called Hatchet Keeper. Whenever the boys played together, if there was a boulder or tree in the way, he would hit it with his stone hatchet and the obstacle would fall to pieces. His hatchet was made of black obsidian.

When the boys became young men they decided to go on a journey to the south. Whenever they came to stones or trees, Hatchet Keeper knocked them aside. When they were hungry, Fast Runner caught an antelope.

After some time they came to a wall of rock which extended to the West and East as far as they could see. They wanted to see over the wall so Fast Runner ran to the East to see where the wall ended. He ran all day and when he returned at nightfall, he told them the wall had no ending. The next day he ran as far as he could to the West, but the wall didn't end there either.

Then Hatchet Keeper tried to break the wall. Again and again he buried his hatchet into the wall. Each time he removed the hatchet, the wall began to crack. In the end, he left some of the hatchet in the wall which became the obsidian found in Yellowstone Park. The wall with the cracks in it became the Rocky Mountains.

The boys then went over the mountains to continue their journey south.

It was during this next adventure that the boys received instructions on how to build the sweat lodge that is so important to Cheyenne tradition.

The boys had extra moccasins with them and so they continued their travels south. At first they saw clouds on the horizon, but soon the country began to change. Water started getting scarce so they traveled at night and rested during the day.

One day they came to a large lake. It looked so inviting they decided to remain there a few days. They drank from the lake and, wandering about, made camp nearby.

One night one of the boys woke up and saw sparks coming from the center of the lake. He woke up the others and as they watched, they became convinced something lived there. And whatever it was, it knew they were there also.

They moved their camp some distance away and went back to sleep. The next morning they returned to the lake to see what may have caused the sparks. Standing at the edge of the water, one of the boys noticed that beautiful shells had washed up on the shore.

One of his friends cautioned, "Don't pick them up until we find out what lives here." Suddenly they saw something in the water; it was so huge they backed away.

A little old man was jumping up and down behind the boys as if he could hardly contain himself. He said, "I've been looking for this animal for a long time. As soon as it comes close, I'm going to catch it."

And that is what he did, jumping in the water to do so. The water began to boil, foam, and turn red. Old man came swimming back, crying out, "I got him, I got him. I finally got him."

He told one of the boys to go toward the blue-looking rocks in the mountains. "Go after your grandmother. Say 'Grandmother, Grandfather has killed that animal he's been looking for for a long time.'"

One of the boys ran to the Blue Stone Mountains. When he arrived there he said, "Grandmother, Grandfather has killed the animal he's been looking for and wants you to bring dogs to pack the meat home."

From among the rocks an old lady came out. She said, "My grandson is here." Grandson replied, "Grandfather wants you to come and bring his dogs."

She called for her dogs, saying it would only take her a little while to get ready. Out of the rocks came big blue-colored dogs.

They all left the mountains and returned to the lake.

In the meantime, the underwater animal had singled out one of the boys and was going to take the spirit from him. The boy already began to smell like underwater moss. This boy was the one who wanted to pick up the pretty shells at the edge of the lake.

Old man said, "I will help you, since you helped me. First I must cut up meat and pack my dogs."

Then he gave instructions on how to build a sweat lodge and taught the boys the purification ceremony which would restore young men to full health. As he instructed them, he also gave them four songs that went with the ceremony.

When they completed the sweat ceremony, they all began to leave, single file, for the mountains. Old man said to the boys, "We eat this kind of animal, but you do not. I will give you some other kind of food to eat."

They arrived in the mountains. The old man and old woman and dogs were happy to have so much food. Old woman cooked other food for the boys.

They stayed in this place for a time, resting up. They had acquired knowledge: how to purify themselves and the use of the sweat lodge.

Once more they continued south.

Preparing for the ceremonial sweat lodge.

The following story tells how the Earth Mother brought both the buffalo and the corn to us.

There were two young men who came into camp, both dressed and painted alike. They began arguing, each accusing the other of copying. Each claimed to have been given the paint by their grandmother, that it was medicine paint with great power. The people thought it was a strange sight, two men dressed and painted alike.

Each of the young men told the villagers that he would prove he was telling the truth and that the other was copying him. They went into the mountains and coming upon a spring, they entered it, walking into a waterfall. Behind the waterfall was a cave, and inside was an old woman sitting by a fire.

She asked the young men, "Why are you arguing and fighting with each other? You have such mean looks on your faces." They both started talking at once, each accusing the other of copying. She told them to be quiet, that she would listen to each in turn.

Each one said they were given the paint and powers by their grandmother, then each asked the old woman, "Give me something to take back to the people so they will know I am telling the truth."

The old woman listened to each, then said, "First you must eat." She gave one young man cooked buffalo meat and the other one cooked corn. She watched as they ate together from the same dishes. They were hungry and ate all that they could, but no matter how much they ate, the dishes remained full.

"I will give each of you a new paint and something to take back to your people to show them you were telling the truth." She gave one young man the dish of buffalo meat and the other the dish of corn. "Feed your people, the Cheyenne, but be sure to feed the orphans and old people first."

The two men emerged from the waterfall, again painted alike (in the future they would fight together as one), but different from when they went in. Each carried a dish of food. When they returned to the village the people ate their fill. When the last of them could eat no more, and all the orphans had been fed, the dishes were empty.

The Cheyenne had many years of good corn crops, and the buffalo were many.

In the mid-1600s many changes came into the lives of our people. We moved to southwestern Minnesota near the Yellow Medicine River. No longer hunters and gatherers, we were farmers who planted fields of corn, beans, and squash. Lodges made from the earth replaced the tepees, and the first permanent village was established.

From our Indian neighbors we acquired the bow and arrow. Our hunters could now go farther into the western prairies to hunt bigger game. The bow and arrow also brought war as tribes became involved in struggles over food and land.

These changes became part of our store of myths, legends, rituals, and ceremonies. Stories were told about the buffalo, the sacred arrows, the prophet Sweet Medicine, and many other areas of life. For us, everything is part of a larger whole.

Everything has meaning. Everything is sacred. As our new stories and ceremonies build upon those that came before, they also draw upon what we learned in the past.

It was while living near the Yellow Medicine River that we first encountered the buffalo. Many of our major legends and rituals about this animal come from this period.

In the beginning the buffalo used to eat humans for food. Despite the bow and arrow that replaced the hunting spear, great buffalo could still say, "We are the most powerful people on Earth." And to the Cheyenne they threw down a challenge: "Let's have a race. The winner will be more powerful than any one of us."

Yellow Whirlwind, a young warrior, accepted the challenge. The buffalo said, "We'll enter the weakest cow in the race, and we'll still beat you." Yellow Whirlwind said, "It's not fair. I have only two legs and the cow has four. I'll get two other legs." But he chose the magpie, saying, "He's got two legs, but he's not going to run on them. He's going to fly."

The animals and birds listened to this confrontation and wanted to be part of it—the wolf, the badger, the meadowlark, the eagle, and the hawk. They believed the buffalo couldn't lose so they said ridiculous things like: "If I lose, I'm going to live in the thorny bushes, and the children will chase me with sticks." "If I lose I'll be this color forever."

The race began and the buffalo took the lead. Only when they had almost completely encircled the Black Hills did the buffalo begin to lag. Still the birds said, "The magpie is the slowest bird there is. I wouldn't worry about it." The magpie kept circling, and after he got so high he swooped down and came in across the finish line ahead of the cow.

After that, the person became more powerful than the buffalo and could eat the buffalo, and the buffalo became a grass-eating animal.

And many of the animals and birds who chose the colors black and white remain so to this day.

One of the ways of calling the buffalo was a four-day ceremony of songs and prayers centered around a round stone. The people took the stone outside and asked a young woman who had not yet known a man to become part of the ceremony. At the end of the four days the buffalo came. It is said that they walked into camp and the people killed them.

Bill Tallbull: "I have seen that stone. It is in the Chicago Museum. For some reason I was led to that place. I began to think of those times long ago when the stone was given to the people who carried it with them. When the buffalo disappeared during the early westward settlement, the stone and the buffalo ceremonies were no longer needed."

Sweet Medicine

One of our major cultural heroes is Sweet Medicine, a prophet, who came to the people in the days when we hunted the buffalo. According to legend, he was called by a great

power to journey into the heart of the Black Hills where it is said he gained much of his wisdom. There he came to the Sacred Mountain, which is now called Bear Butte. He entered a lodge where old men were sitting along one side and old women along the other. They were really spirits, not people, and they called him Grandson and taught him many things to take back to his people.

Sweet Medicine saw four arrows in the lodge, and the old ones taught him first about these, because they were to become the tribe's highest source of power. They told him, "Two are for hunting, and two are for war."

If one Cheyenne ever kills another, the arrows (now tainted, blood-specked) must be renewed in the Sacred Arrow Renewal Ceremony. In this way, the anger of the killing is washed away. The entire Cheyenne tribe is cleansed, and the power of the Sacred Arrows is renewed.

By tradition, Sweet Medicine also brought us our laws and government which helped us flourish as a people.

This government was led by forty-four chiefs called the Council of Forty-Four. Each chief represented one of the Cheyenne bands and was the head of an extended family made up of his wife, children, aunts, uncles, and the elders. The Council was responsible for settling disputes and for deciding when it was time to move the camp. It made

Prayer cloths and symbols of faith at Bear Butte.

decisions about tribal war policy and alliances with other tribes. The chiefs were concerned with the well-being of both the tribe and the individuals in it, and they often made sacrifices to help others. Their characteristic traits served as a model for other Cheyennes: wisdom, calmness, stability, kindliness, fairness, selflessness, generosity, energy, and bravery. (Carl Waldman, *Encyclopedia of Native American Tribes*, Facts On File Publications, New York, 1988, p. 49.)

Today the Cheyenne people have a tribal government with a constitution and bylaws. All enrolled tribal members of voting age elect the tribal president, vice president, and ten Tribal Council members. Residents of each of the five voting districts——Busby, Birney, Lame Deer, Ashland, and Muddy—elect council members.

Our four military societies come from Sweet Medicine too. Societies were made up of warriors from different bands organized into four groups: the Swift Foxes (or Kit Foxes), Elks, Red Shields, and Bow Strings. These warriors fought together and carried out raids on other tribes. They made plans for military campaigns. The societies were also clubs that had their own traditions with its rituals, sacred objects, symbols, and articles of clothing. Later, other military societies developed, including the Dog, Wolf, and Crazy Dogs. (Waldman, pp. 49-50.)

One of the toys children still play with today to make them healthy and strong is the hoop made out of buffalo hide. According to legend, it came to us from Sweet Medicine, when he went out hunting for food.

It was a difficult time. The people had been camped in the village for some time, and the men had hunted without finding any game. They had eaten all the dried meat and fruit.

Sweet Medicine's grandmother gave him some wild turnips which were all she had left. He asked her, "Can you bring me a buffalo hide? I want to use it to make a hoop and I'll show you what to do."

Grandmother looked and looked and finally found a calf hide. Sweet Medicine told her to soak it in the river for four days. Then he added, "Get a straight cherrywood bough and trim and shape it into a hoop. Tie it with a buckskin string and hang it in the sun to dry. Make four pointed sticks of cherrywood and dry them in the sun also."

After Grandmother had done all these things, Sweet Medicine showed her how to weave the string back and forth to make a net with a hole in the middle. Then they painted the net and the four cherrywood throwing sticks with paint made from the red earth.

The next morning they went to the village, and soon a group of people gathered around them. Grandmother held the hoop as Sweet Medicine picked up one of the throwing sticks, threw it, hit the hoop, and knocked it over. Then he pulled out the stick, laid it on the ground, gave the hoop back to his Grandmother and threw another stick at the hoop while she rolled it. A third time he did the same thing.

The fourth time he threw the stick it went through the round hole in the center of the hoop. This time the hoop did not turn over. Instead it turned into a live buffalo calf with an arrow in its side. It staggered around several times until it fell over.

Then Sweet Medicine removed the arrow and said to the people, "Come get your meat." There was plenty for everyone and even much left over.

Cheyenne beliefs

We are a very spiritual people, and we developed our system of beliefs about the Creator from those days on the Plains and our early history. From generation to generation we passed these beliefs on. In our traditional Cheyenne language, the name for the Creator is Maheo, sometimes called the All Father. These are some of our beliefs:

We believe there is only One who created everything, who created life. The old priests used to tell us this. Maheo is so great, we cannot fully describe Him. Though we have never seen Him, we know Him as the God over all.

We believe Maheo and the Sacred Powers give us great supernatural power for life and that the world we live in is basically good.

We believe that creation is a constantly changing, dynamic system in which all the parts are interrelated and form one harmonious whole. Thus all are united in a single living unity.

We believe the source of this unity is Maheo and therefore mysterious and divine.

We believe that Maheo shares His divine life and power with us through the four Sacred Arrows, also called the Mahuts. He also shares His power with certain Sacred Persons, the priests of our tribe, and with other lesser powers such as the animals that are so important to us.

Our sacred ceremonies are a way we draw upon this power. We believe it is important to have these ceremonies and draw upon this power because our people and the world need to be continually renewed. Our most important ceremonies are:

> The Sacred Arrow rites, which draw upon the power of Maheo to renew the Cheyenne as a people.
>
> The New Life Lodge or Sun Dance ceremony, which brings renewed life to the world and everyone in it.
>
> The Sacred Buffalo Hat ceremony, which generates power to renew and attract the buffalo as a source of food and life.

Whenever there is disorder in the world, we believe that offering a sacred ceremony serves to restore harmony and vitality; creation works smoothly and people stay well and survive.

We believe it is important to share and sacrifice for the benefit of one another.

The chapel at St. Labre Indian School.

In turn, through sacrifice, both men and women draw upon the supernatural power of the universe. Life continues through the act of sharing in procreation which is a form of sacrifice. This is so because reproductive power is a limited energy and should not be wasted but used carefully for the good of the family and the continuation of the tribe. This is why we bless this act through sacred ceremonies.

We believe that both men and women have their own sacred power. The four Sacred Arrows are the sacred symbol of male power, while the Sacred Buffalo Hat is the symbol of female power.

Women have always been influential and important in Cheyenne life. We believe that the woman is above everything, because Maheo has given her the power to give birth. So she has the power to spread people to cover the earth.

Women have always freely discussed tribal affairs with their husbands and have great influence in what they do. According to tradition, a woman founded the Council of Forty-Four which Sweet Medicine brought to the people. Some women have possessed powers as healers and medicine women.

The chastity of Cheyenne women before marriage is considered extremely important. A woman is honored and respected for her chastity, and this is reflected in the holiness of the woman's sacrificial role in tribal ceremonies as Sacred Woman. We believe, as stated by one of our priests, Fire Wolf, "Out of man, the woman was first made by Maheo. Through her, the earth and the people of the earth are replenished."

We believe all things are sacred, and we repeatedly honor this through our sacred ceremonies. We believe that under the one Supreme Being, Maheo, there are four Sacred Persons who live at the four cardinal points of the universe, represented by the four directions.

We honor Grandmother Earth as a living, supernatural being. We honor and call on the Above and Below Persons for blessings. These include the Sun, Thunder, Moon, Morning Star and Stars, the Whirlwind, and the Badger. We honor and call upon the aid of the lesser Sacred Powers who appear in the form of animals, birds, and natural phenomena such as storms and lightning.

Sacred ceremonies

Many of our ceremonies still observed today come from the time when we were on the Plains and followed the buffalo. In the early 1800s we joined forces with a neighboring group of people, the Suhtaio or Buffalo People, who introduced us to many ceremonies related to calling and renewing these animals. By the 1830s we had united as one tribe.

Our ceremonies and celebrations became larger too. Some were new, others were adapted from earlier times when we first moved out onto the prairies.

Since the Cheyenne are made up of two related tribes, Suhtaio and Tsistsistas, they have two cultural heroes and two mysterious objects—the Medicine Arrows (Mahuts) and the Sacred Buffalo Hat (Issiwun). All these mysteries and ceremonies they learned from the spirits that they encountered in the underground lodges within the earth.

The *Arrow Renewal* ceremony, given to us by the prophet, Sweet Medicine, is the highest ceremonial belief in Cheyenne ceremonial belief hierarchy. By renewing the arrows, the ceremony renewed the tribe, as Sweet Medicine taught us. It was performed in the years when the Cheyenne bands came together.

During the year the Sacred Arrows were kept in a medicine bundle in a special tepee. At the time of the ceremony, the arrows were placed in the Sacred Arrow Lodge which stood in the center of a circle with two other lodges, the Sacred Arrow Keeper's Lodge and the Offering Lodge. Around the circle were the tepees of all the Cheyenne bands, originally ten.

During the four days of the ceremony, the Sacred Arrow Keeper and other male participants from each of the bands performed a series of rituals to renew the Sacred Arrows, thereby renewing the tribe. Only the pledger performed the ritual of renewing according to the rules of the instructor, who ensured the sacredness of the ceremony. Other men secured and patrolled the camp.

The *Medicine Lodge* or *Sun Dance* ceremony was a renewal ceremony that lasted five days and began with preparations, instruction of the dancers, and erecting of the lodge. It was a highly spiritual occasion during which participants performed the Sun Dance, each for a specific purpose such as paying back a vow made to the great powers, to seek a blessing, to support a friend who may be paying his vow, or to show loyalty to one's soldier band.

Ritual ceremonies were performed during the building of the Medicine Lodge. Priests—old men familiar with the ceremony—came together with instructors who were to teach the secrets of the ceremony, and with the instructors' assistants. Women, although they did not dance, took part in the ceremonies. The Medicine Lodge could be

offered by either a man or a woman; however, if vowed by a woman, her husband danced for her.

In the old days an Indian brave would pledge an offering to the great powers to gain favor, whether to satisfy a desire or to ward off impending disaster. To honor a pledge, a sacrifice was promised. This sometimes took the form of body piercing, a ritual which was banned for a time (but is still performed today), its spiritual significance misunderstood by non-Indians who objected to its practice.

Dancers who participated in the Sun Dance received assistance from the instructors with body painting. Dancers were hail-painted, that is, painted with large white circles. Others might be painted to represent animals such as the deer or eagle. (George Bird Grinnell, *The Cheyenne Indians: Their History and Ways of Life*, Vol. 2., University of Nebraska Press, Lincoln and London, 1972, pp. 212–284.)

The *Animal Dance* or *Massaum* ceremony is also known as the Buffalo Dance or Crazy Dance. It is said to have been brought to the tribe by one of two similarly dressed young men who went into the earth and brought out food.

The Massaum ceremony lasted for five days and was designed to help our hunters find food to feed the people. The first four days were one of preparation. Some members of the tribe prepared and painted a wolf skin for the pledger to wear. Others participated in building a corral where the dance would take place. Women as well as men helped in preparing for this event, unlike the Arrow Renewal ceremony which was participated in by men only.

On the fifth day everyone became a part of the ceremony. The warriors dressed up as animals and the members of the Bowstring Society pretended to hunt and herd them into the corral. Once they had them there, the warriors began to dance. But instead of dancing forward, they danced backwards, and everyone else clowned around. It was fun for the spectators as well as the dancers. Because of their crazy behavior, the Bowstring Society was called the Contrary Society, while the Animal Dance became known as the Crazy Dance.

Winter

I wince at the sound of my name
And hold the tears from my face
At times I want to hang my head in shame
All because of feelings toward my race.

I lose sleep at night
Never wanting to be alone
Constantly wondering what's right
Although racism is one thing I'll never condone.

I have large dreams of fortune and fame
Which may never come true
There are several to blame
For the bitterness, but least of all you.

It is a silent fight
Forever monotone
A wrong which will never be right
Until the pain is sewn.

The period of the next hundred years, 1800–1900, was a dark winter for the Cheyenne people. It was the period of history when contact with the white man altered forever the American Indian way of life.

One of the great Cheyenne chiefs, Highchief, spoke eloquently of what these times foretold.

Once, only Indians lived in this land. Then came strangers from across the Great Water. No land had they; we gave them our land. No food had they; we gave them of our corn. The strangers are becoming many and they fill all the country. They dig gold from my mountains; they build houses of the trees of my forests; they rear cities of my stones and rocks; they make fine garments from the hides of animals that eat my grass. None of the things that make their riches did they bring with them from beyond the Great Water; all comes from my land, the land the Great Mystery gave unto the Indian.

And when I think upon this, I know that it is right, even this. In the heart of the Great Mystery it was meant that strangers/visitors—my friends across the Great Water—should come to my land; that I should bid them welcome; that all men should sit down with me and eat together of my corn. It was meant by the Great Mystery that the Indian should give to all people.

Following is a description of this sad time, and tells how, in spite of all their sorrow and suffering, the Northern Cheyenne people managed to survive and go on.

The Cheyennes first contact with white men occurred at the end of the 1700s after they had moved to the Missouri River and begun to hunt buffalo on the Plains. By this time they had acquired the horse from another friendly tribe. The horse granted an independence that the Cheyennes had never known before.

Lucille Spear, Cheyenne elder, tells about these times.

The introduction of the horse furnished to all the Plains tribes a new and strong motive for war, for by war men might acquire something of very great value. Until the coming of the horse, the only possessions of the Plains Indians, except for food and clothing, were their dogs, weapons, and implements of stone, wood, and bone.

The horse's usefulness was at once recognized, for here was an animal whose possession added immensely to the comfort and freedom of the people: it carried them and their families wherever they pleased and revealed a means of discovering and venturing into new areas of the country previously unknown. The horse permitted the pursuit and capture of game and helped in the transportation of household goods over long distances from one camp to another.

Only two ways of procuring horses of any number were known: by capturing wild horses on the prairie or those in possession of neighboring tribes. The practice of taking horses from the enemy became a regular profession among the Cheyennes.

The Cheyenne had now moved out onto the Plains in large numbers to hunt the buffalo as a way of life; others remained in villages growing crops.

In 1803 the United States concluded the Louisiana Purchase with France, laying claim to a vast territory from the Gulf of Mexico to the Canadian border and from the Mississippi River west to the Rocky Mountains. It included the land of the Cheyenne.

Like other Indian tribes, the Cheyenne never considered this land something one owns. For them, it was like one's mother or grandmother, which is why they called the land Grandmother Earth. But now the Americans believed they owned this land that they had bought from the French, and they soon sent explorers and then traders and settlers into Indian territory.

The first Cheyenne exchange of goods with white men was made initially through neighboring tribes, the Arikaras and Mandans, who were trading for European goods and agricultural products. Direct contact soon followed.

The first to come were Meriwether Lewis and William Clark, who led their famous expedition from St. Louis through the Louisiana Territory from 1804 to 1806. The Cheyenne were camped in the Black Hills in 1806 when Lewis and Clark came upon them. These were friendly meetings, but one Cheyenne chief sensed the danger to come.

Clark, in an act of friendship, tried to present this chief with an American medal. The chief refused to accept it, telling Clark that he knew of the white people's medicine, that he was afraid of the medal or anything that white people gave them.

At Clark's persuasion, the chief finally accepted the medal. It was a warning of what lay ahead, as the white men continued to come and urge upon the Cheyenne what they were afraid of and did not want.

Following Lewis and Clark, more white men came, mostly traders, but others were scientists and naturalists, such as John Bradbury, English botanist, who wanted to learn about Cheyenne plant lore.

Grace Strangeowl

The knowledge of plants used as medicine has a long history in Cheyenne tradition. Bill Tallbull remembers a time when the teaching of plants was still a vital part of Cheyenne Indian life.

During the summer of 1928 when I was eight years old, I lived with my grandparents at their log cabin on Muddy Creek. It was about the middle of June when a man rode into our yard asking for my grandmother, saying he had been sent on behalf of a cancer patient. My grandmother specialized in the treatment of cancer, and he was referring to a particular medicine that she had.

This was the beginning of my grandmother's teaching of plants. The names of these plants was the first lesson passed on to us. Identity of the plants was next and where they could be found, how they were picked, and later how they were prepared for use. The taking of a plant had been established long ago, and treatment of this plant during plant picking time was sacred. Being very careful of the treatment of medicine plants was as important as applying or dispensing medicine to a patient.

Some plants were picked in the middle of the day and some were picked only when there were no clouds in the sky. Medicine men and women picked certain plants and also certain amounts. Other people sometimes picked plants for them, and sometimes certain plants were only picked by children. Many prayers and tobacco were offered to plants during this time.

Plants were used in Cheyenne renewal ceremonies. Our people developed strong spiritual relationships with plants and called them our friends. These relationships exist to this day.

The plant lore of the Cheyenne Indians was nearly lost until Tallbull revived the tradition at the Dull Knife Memorial College, where he "set about studying and preserving for my peoples this lore."

During the early 19th century the pressure on the Cheyenne gradually built as more white traders came, and as they fought more with other tribes over the profits to be made from trading and over the land where tribes hunted and raised crops for trade. By now many tribes had guns, turning them into warriors.

As the white traders began to set up trading posts and forts, the soldiers arrived to

protect them. The Cheyenne continued to hunt the buffalo and to do business with traders, even signing their first treaty of friendship with the United States as a trading partner. The Cheyenne had great hope that all could live together in peace, trading and helping each other. But as they soon discovered, this was not to be.

Despite some problems, mostly due to horse raiding, by 1840 the Cheyenne were still generally friendly with the whites. But during those years the problems increased, as the United States expanded its territory throughout the West, and more and more settlers moved through Indian lands, killing the buffalo.

Along with trade, the settlers brought disease. Measles, whooping cough, and cholera ravaged the Cheyenne people who, having no immunity to these diseases, were decimated, with half their community being wiped out.

Alcohol was brought to the Plains by traders and the military. The Indians were attracted to alcohol for numerous reasons: the immediate effects of alcohol produced a magical introduction of visions, hallucinations, and delusions similar to those achievable through the difficult Vision Quest which included exposure, time, hunger, thirst, and dedication. Compared to the process and procedures for achieving this transforming state in the traditional manner, the simulated, mind-altering effects of alcohol were virtually instantaneous.

Since the Cheyenne people had no history with alcohol, they had no inhibitions or cultural restraints to help them resist the negative effects. Consequently, many became dependent, and this dependence was exploited by traders and shopkeepers around the forts and settlements with Indians performing the most menial and degrading tasks.

The most destructive aftermath of alcohol on the Indian way of life was how its effects changed priorities, values, and behaviors from tribal and community integrity to personal and individual self-gratification: the people became Indians as opposed to tribal members, that is, Cheyenne, Sioux, Crow, etc.

By the 1850s the siege of disease was over but the attack on the culture and hearts of the Cheyenne continued to increase. Campsites were desecrated as settlers used them for their own, not understanding that these sites were sacred to the Indians, who were now prevented from using them. Worse was the decline of the buffalo, so central to Cheyenne culture. Settlers slaughtered the buffalo or drove them away from their grazing lands, so that the animals began to change their migration patterns and were difficult to find.

It was clear that the settlers, soldiers, and other white men saw the Indian as a barrier in the way of their settlements; they did not understand what all the things that were lost to the Cheyenne meant to them.

During the years 1851-1868, a number of treaties were signed between bands of Indian tribes and the US government. Unfortunately for the Indians, these treaties gave the government the right to continue building forts and roads, often in and through Indian territory that had been assigned to them, land that kept shrinking with each major treaty.

These contracts between the Indians and the US government were "sealed" by the ceremonial offering of the peace pipe.

Lucille Spear explains how the offering of the pipe in Cheyenne tradition exemplifies the most sacred trust between any two parties entering into an agreement.

The offering of the pipe was not confined to war matters. The pipe was and is the ceremonial method of requesting any favor of importance. The acceptance and smoking of the offered pipe is a favorable answer to the request. The Cheyenne have a strong belief in the offering of the pipe, accepting the pipe, smoking the pipe, which confirms and carries out the vow, pledge, or request for favor. The pipe is smoked in truth and honesty and is a great spiritual communication with our Creator.

Each time a band of the Cheyenne signed another treaty, they kept hoping it would be the final one, that now the white Americans would be satisfied, and they could all live in peace. But each time they felt a little more sadness and despair.

By the mid-1860s, the fight for the Cheyenne homeland became more and more desperate. For those battles that were won, many were lost. One of the most devastating for the Cheyenne was the Sand Creek Massacre of 1864.

Bill Tallbull tells the story.

White settlers living on the Plains were becoming nervous because they knew the Indian tribes were increasingly restless and aggressive. One event that particularly unnerved them was an uprising by the Sioux in Minnesota in 1862 in which a number of whites were killed. So rumors spread throughout the Plains, including Colorado, that the Southern Cheyenne planned to move north to ally with the Northern Cheyenne and Sioux to attack settlements on the frontier.

Plenty Horses, Cheyenne, May 10, 1875

In response, Colonel John M. Chivington, who headed up the Colorado Volunteers, organized a force to go out and "kill Cheyennes whenever and wherever they are found." And that's what happened that fateful night in November 1864. About 500 Southern Cheyenne, who were friendly with whites, were camped on Sand Creek close to their reservation. About two-thirds of the group were women and children. The group made their camp here because Black Kettle, their leader—one of three Southern Cheyenne chiefs who had signed the 1861 Treaty of Fort Wise—had been assured by the army officers that they would not be attacked. Chief Black Kettle even ran up an American flag and a white banner on a pole to let the troops know the group was friendly.

As the sun came up on November 29, Chivington and 700 Colorado Volunteers stormed into their camp trying to kill everyone they could—men, women, children, even pregnant women, it didn't matter. When it was over, 137 people were dead, over 100 of them women and children.

In response, there was one of the biggest Indian uprisings with about 2000 warriors conducting raids against wagon trains, stage stations, homesteads, and military posts along the South Platte River.

For a few more years we had some more successful battles, though it was only a matter of time before the tide turned against us.

The Fetterman Fight of 1866 was one such successful battle. It led to the Treaty of 1868 which set aside land for the Indians, although that treaty, too, was breached.

Bill Tallbull describes how the Fetterman Fight came about.

Cheyenne Indian warriors had twice attacked Fort Phil Kearny between the Tongue and Powder Rivers in what is now Wyoming. The Cheyenne chief, Little Wolf, along with Sioux chiefs Crazy Horse and Buffalo Hump, realized they couldn't defeat the fort itself. Instead, under their plan a group of Cheyennes, Sioux, and Arapahos attacked a wagon train of men sent out by the fort to cut wood.

Following the attack, Captain William J. Fetterman was dispatched with 81 officers to come to the aid of the wagon train. But Fetterman, who had only recently arrived at the fort, was new to Indian fighting. As a result, though his commander, Colonel Carrington, had warned him to avoid going beyond the Lodge Ridge Trail near the wagons because of the possibility of ambush, Fetterman did anyway. A few Indian warriors rode up as decoys

Robert Ridge Walker, Northern Cheyenne, 1888–1897

and Fetterman and his men rode after them. It was a fatal mistake. The decoys led the soldiers well into the trap where 2000 warriors awaited them—the Cheyenne and Arapaho on one side and the Sioux on the other. Fetterman and all of his men were killed.

The entire nation was shocked because for the first time Indians had completely destroyed a US military detachment. So while the Indians savored their sweet victory, the anger of the US government against them intensified.

After the Fetterman Fight and the Treaty of 1868, there was a time of brief peace. But it was an uncomfortable one with much distrust on both sides. While some Cheyennes and other Plains Indians now lived on the Great Sioux Reservation in South Dakota and received rations from the US government, others continued to live and hunt in the Powder River country, though they too received supplies from the government.

Meanwhile, frontiersmen and miners continued to cross into Indian lands while the government continued to build more forts. By the mid-1870s more battles broke out again, culminating in the Battle of Little Bighorn in June 1876.

This battle has been told again and again in written word and on film. Lucille Spear has a somewhat different perspective than the one generally accepted by the masses.

Custer [General George Armstrong Custer] smoked with the Cheyenne chiefs, and one of the medicine men told him, "Now you're smoking our peace pipe. We smoke this in peace. We honor peace, and we are asking you not to make war on us anymore. But if you don't keep your word, you will be no more on this earth."

Time went on and Custer attacked the Cheyenne camp again. And after that there were a lot more incidents. So members of the Sioux, Arapaho, and the Cheyenne came together for a meeting along the Tongue River. Then they all moved their camps there.

Custer came with his troops. He was the one who broke his word, and he led his soldiers to slaughter, and that's how it was. But the white people, they have their own version.

After the Battle of Little Bighorn, the position of the US government toward the Indians hardened, so that by the fall of 1877 some bands of Cheyenne and Sioux had agreed to give up most of their lands including the Black Hills and surrounding area—land long held sacred to the Indians.

In the months following, most bands of Cheyenne and Sioux off the reservation surrendered. Some bands of Cheyenne were sent to Fort Keogh, an agency by the confluence of the Yellowstone and Tongue Rivers in southeastern Montana. Several bands of Cheyenne were sent to northern Nebraska and subsequently on to a reservation in Oklahoma.

The Trek

For the 1000 Northern Cheyenne living on the reservation in Oklahoma, life was unbearable. Unaccustomed to the hot, humid weather and exposed to disease, many came down with malaria. Medical supplies were few and many died. Others starved to death, mostly women and children.

A year of this extreme deprivation passed. Spurred on by their people, Chiefs Dull Knife and Little Wolf went to the Indian agent, asking that the Cheyennes be allowed to return to their home in the North. Little Wolf made an eloquent plea:

> My people were raised there, in a land of pines and clear, cold rivers. There we were always healthy for there was meat enough for all. We were happy until the Great Father's soldiers brought us here.
>
> This is not a good place for us. There is too much heat and not enough food. We wish to return to our home in the mountains.

Their request was refused. But this decision was unacceptable to the Cheyennes. "If we stay, we all die. Let us die fighting to reach our homeland." This was the sentiment expressed by most.

It was decided. They would go home, with or without the government's permission.

So on September 9, 1878 the Northern Cheyenne left Oklahoma. There were 300 of them with less than 80 warriors; 13,000 troops mobilized against them.

Lucille Spear's great-grandmother with her children and grandchildren (one of whom was Spear's father) was among the Northern Cheyenne held on the Oklahoma

reservation. She relates the story of the Cheyennes' trek back to the North as she heard it from her family.

They had a few horses. Sometimes they walked, and sometimes they'd hide until nightfall and start out then, always with the dust of the soldiers right behind them. They got very hungry, so hungry they couldn't feel it anymore....

One time they were hiding in a ditch beside a railroad track. The train came by and they all squatted down. The train slowed, and this man wearing a white cap and white shirt threw a big bundle out the window. It was bread. Why did he do this? They didn't know, but he must have had a reason.

Soon after that the soldiers were very near. The Cheyennes came upon a meadow with small hills and no place to hide. They could see that dust coming from behind, and there were the soldiers and their volunteers. My grandma said, "They're not going to catch us, don't be afraid." One of the Cheyenne riders rode up and down, calling out, "Everybody stop and listen. Just stand where you are. We are going to take out our medicine bundles and smoke." They all did as they were told, and the medicine man and the chiefs prayed that they would get home safely.

Then one of the men took a stick and drew a line on the ground. He told everyone to walk across it very slowly but to let the children run if they wanted to. So that's what they did.

When the soldiers came upon them, they went to where the line was drawn. They couldn't find any tracks, so they rode up and down, thinking that the Cheyennes must be hiding somewhere. Then they saw a small herd of buffalo grazing and moving slowly away from them. They saw these little buffalo calves trying to follow them and playing. It was the children. To the soldiers' eyes they saw buffalo, but it was actually the Cheyennes. That's how strong their medicine was.

Then it started snowing, and the older women who had blankets, some of them ragged, made strips out of them and wrapped the children's feet to keep them warm.

And some Cheyennes wanted to go only as far as Red Cloud Agency, saying, "We'll get shelter there. The children are tired and hungry. If we continue, they might freeze or die of starvation."

That was Dull Knife's argument. But the younger men wanted to keep going, saying, "We can make it. We know that country. There's game over there. We'll find a good place to hide."

Standing at his grandfather's grave, Cordell Little Coyote Backbone becomes a hereditary chief and member of the Council of 44, at the age of eight.

But Dull Knife was determined to save the children, the women, and the old people. So the Cheyennes split up with Dull Knife's group heading toward Red Cloud Agency and Little Wolf taking most of the braves with him.

In a snowstorm—exhausted, hungry, and near freezing—Dull Knife and his party were halfway between Red Cloud Agency and Fort Robinson when they were surrounded and disarmed by soldiers, taken to the fort, and housed in abandoned barracks.

In late December word came from Washington that the Indians were to be sent back to Oklahoma.

But the Cheyennes had made it this far and sacrificed too much to submit to this humiliation. They refused to return to Oklahoma. Their refusal brought down upon them the harshest of penalties: all water, food, and heat were cut off. But even this inhuman punishment imposed upon them in the dead of winter only strengthened their resolve.

Lucille Spear tells how the Cheyenne people had prepared themselves for this final flight to their homeland.

At the time the Cheyennes made the decision to go to Red Cloud Agency, they had taken five rifles apart and hidden them among the children's things. My father says that shells were put into a necklace he was wearing. Other rifle parts were hidden in the splints on my uncle's broken leg. So now they reassembled those rifles and prepared to break out of Fort Robinson and head for home.

My uncle said, "I cannot run because of my leg. I will leave with you, but I'm going to stake myself in the snow and I will die there fighting." So he went outside and with a leather thong staked himself in the snow. According to the Dog Soldiers, when you stake yourself, you must stay and fight. And if you survive and the enemy is beaten, then you can take the stake out.

Ted Risingsun, Cheyenne elder, was the great-grandson of Chief Dull Knife. His grandmother was a survivor of the tragedy that occurred on the night of January 8, 1879 at Fort Robinson, Nebraska Territory. Dull Knife's band escaped from the prison barracks after suffering many cruel days imprisoned without water, fuel, or food. The temperature had fallen to forty below zero. Most of these people were elderly women, small children, and pregnant mothers, frantic from hunger and thirst.

Ted Risingsun recalls the story his grandmother often told of her desperate escape.

As she ran from the barracks under heavy gunfire, she picked up her four-year-old sister and placed her on her shoulders. Suddenly, she was hit from behind with a bullet to her head. She fell wounded in the snow but did not lose consciousness.

"Follow them! You know where they went!" she screamed at her little sister. The child ran off into the night. As she lay there preparing to die, a remarkable thing happened. A courageous soldier stood in front of the terrified girl to shield her from his troop's gunfire. That soldier saved her life. My grandmother never forgot this kindness.

The US government, having learned of their march from Oklahoma and moved by all that the Cheyennes had endured, agreed that they could remain in the North. Of the original 300 who had left Oklahoma, the Cheyenne people now numbered between 90 and 100.

Ted Risingsun's last wish was that his people never forget to tell the Cheyenne youth where they came from and what price their ancestors paid to have this piece of land that is now their home. "Take care of it because this is the last place the Northern Cheyenne have to call home. This land was paid for by the blood of our ancestors."

This tragic episode in Cheyenne history is often referred to as The Last Stand or The Defeat. But Rubie Sooktis, board member of the Dull Knife Memorial Foundation sees it differently:

Much of what I know of Cheyenne history—my own family history of the tribe—has been passed down orally. What I see as the Cheyenne outbreak at Fort Robinson is the determination of a small group of people against impossible odds. I think you can define it as the strength of the people who were starved, who were prisoners at Fort Robinson, who resisted returning to Oklahoma. It was defined with their lives, with that unbelievable determination.

The long struggle was over. The Cheyennes had survived. Now began a new life on the reservation.

Spring

Forever Last

Nothing will forever last
Except the earth and sky
I hope to look on my past
And remember the love between you and I.

It burns too intense
A fire ablaze
I have no defense
From the sparks in your gaze.

In the universe so vast
Our love can only intensify
Though I'm still an outcast
And on you I rely.

We all start with innocence
Then love brings a haze
Which seems to condense
And leave us in a daze.

The white man never has known the Indian. It is thus: there are two roads, the white man's road, and the Indian's road. Neither traveler knows the road of the other. Thus ever has it been, from long ago, even unto today.

Chief Highchief

From here on the history of the Cheyenne is our story and describes how the earlier battles for our homes and the lives of our people now became battles of survival within the limited boundaries of the reservation.

Yet somehow in those troubled days we did survive, preserving most of our culture. And despite those difficult times, we began the slow process of planting new seeds for the future, seeds that would take many years to germinate, so barren and rocky was the soil.

But we did what we could to plant them—from the darkest and coldest days of early spring, to the warmer, brighter days when hope began to blossom once more.

Learning to adapt to a new way of life

By the late 1890s the scattered bands of the Northern Cheyenne were reunited on the Tongue River Reservation in southeastern Montana, initially 371,200 acres of valley and high plains grassland surrounded by three divides. This land would become our permanent settlement to be renamed the Northern Cheyenne Reservation.

Our first years on the reservation were marked by hunger and poverty. We lost many of our people. We had little to wear. Most of our horses had either been killed or taken by the US Army. We did some hunting, though game was limited to small animals such as deer and rabbits. Men and women learned how to raise gardens. We also learned how to use a walking plow and horses to plant crops, although our first experience with the plow resulted in an early setback. It happened this way:

An agent and a government farmer went to the home of one Cheyenne to teach him to plow. A group of other Cheyennes gathered to watch the lesson and learn too. They thought it would be easy, as they harnessed the two horses and hooked them up to a walking plow. But then as they started moving down the field, with one Cheyenne driving the team and the other holding the plow, they suddenly plowed up two bull snakes.

Now the snake is considered a dangerous, untrustworthy animal. So the two Cheyennes stopped plowing, saying they didn't want to go on. However, the agent and government farmer were able to persuade two more Cheyennes to try.

Cheyenne Agency, Lame Deer, Mt. 1904

Ted Risingsun

But this time those two plowed up a rattlesnake. It began hissing angrily at them. At this point, none of the Indians were willing to plow anymore. As one said: "We might plow up something that will really get after us! This is just showing we shouldn't turn the earth upside down."

And so they all went home and there was no more plowing that day.

Eventually, we did learn to plow. But the farming effort was not very successful. As a result, we had to turn to the rations provided by the Bureau of Indian Affairs (BIA). These included beans, coffee, sugar, and beef. But often we didn't receive enough to last from ration day to ration day, so the people went hungry. To supplement our meager diet, hunters went searching for game off the reservation, and sometimes they shot a cow of a neighboring white rancher. But this only led to conflicts.

Many of our warriors became scouts for the US soldiers, surveying and developing the surrounding territory, which included clearing brush and making trails for the settlers and ranchers who continued to come in high numbers.

The US government decided the best approach to "civilizing" the Indians was to make us like the white man, and the best way to accomplish this was through education. So we were required by law to send our children to American schools. This often meant boarding schools, some as far away as Carlisle, Pennsylvania, and for years at a time.

Of all our troubles, the separation from our children was the hardest to bear.

Ted Risingsun recalls this time.

At six years of age every Cheyenne child was expected in school. If the children did not go to school, then the family did not get their rations. We had nothing to say about how the school was run, what would be taught there, who would do the teaching. All this was decided by the Bureau.

Bill Tallbull remembers his school experience.

Having gone to school, having run away from school, trying to adjust to the way they wanted me to be, I often asked myself: "Who am I going to be? Who do you want me to be?" The teachers said, "We want you to learn the values of middle-class America." I wondered what those values were. Were they good values? I took those values and

compared them with the spiritual values of my people, and they were at odds with each other . . .

It was not until the 1960s when a tribal school board was created that we were allowed a say in our children's education.

We realized we had to adapt to the white man's ways in order to survive, that for the sake of the children we had no choice. Yet we also wanted to maintain many of our own ways. We believed that, in spite of the bleakness of our new life, if we strove to preserve our cultural traditions, we would endure. The teachings that helped us then are still being taught today:

You have to believe in something. Nothing in this world is going to help.

In prayer, you learn to pray for everybody.

Sometimes we forget to ask for help. Animals, flowers, plants are a part of us.

We have to learn to support each other. You get things, you give things back.

Put enough wings on the problem, and pretty soon it is gone.

Though life was hard, we kept up our spirits and learned to adapt. In fact, we appeared to succeed so well that the cavalry soldiers were impressed with our determination. Lieutenant William Philo Clark of the Second Cavalry, whom we called White Hat, showed his respect and sympathy for us with these words:

The men of the Cheyenne Indians rank as high in the scale of honesty, energy, and tenacity of purpose as those of any other tribe I have met, and in physique and intellect they are superior to most tribes and the equal of any. Under the most demoralizing and trying circumstances they have preserved to a remarkable degree that part of their moral code which relates to chastity, and public sentiment has been so strong in them in regard to this matter that they have been, and still are, noted among all the tribes which surround them for the virtue of their women.

Continuing conflicts between the Cheyenne and the white settlers over land disputes led to the Executive Order of 1884 which stated that the land set aside for the reservation was "for the use and occupation of the Northern Cheyenne Indians...and such other Indians as the Secretary of the Interior may see fit to locate thereon."

Unfortunately, there was one big problem. The white homesteaders who had already settled on lands within the reservation boundaries could stay there, as could those who had made claims to these lands. Thus, both Indians and settlers were intermixed on the reservation in a "checkerboard" pattern. This was thought by the Indian Bureau to be a good idea because living among whites would civilize us. But instead, the presence of these homesteaders and ranchers only contributed to further conflicts.

One of these confrontations concerned the burning of the Alderson cabin in 1884.

John Stands In Timber tells the story.

My father, Stands Different, was one of four Cheyennes who served prison terms for what happened. It took place the year I was born, the same year the reservation was established.

Among the early white settlers who had taken up land was Walt Alderson who had a ranch at the place now called Alderson Gulch at the present agency in Lame Deer. When the trouble arose he was away from home.

Several of Alderson's cowboys were working at the ranch when Chief Black Wolf passed through about noon while on a visiting trip. The cowboys were cooking dinner, and they offered him a plate of food. Grateful to get it, Black Wolf sat on the grass in the shade, and after he finished eating he fell asleep.

He was wearing one of those tall black hats. One of the cowboys took out a six-shooter and said: "I bet I can knock off that hat and not hit him." The others told him not to—he might kill him. But the cowboy shot anyway, creasing Black Wolf's skull, and the old man fell down, unconscious. The cowboys, thinking they had killed him, got on their horses and beat it.

Eventually Black Wolf got up, but when he started walking he said the earth seemed to turn under him and he fell over. He finally gave up trying to walk, found the trail and just crawled. Someone from the village found him and took him in on horseback. Of course, they all thought the white man had tried to kill him.

A war party was organized, but by the time the Indians got to the ranch it was deserted, so they rode in, shot the windows out, broke in, took everything they wanted, and set the house on fire. When they got through there was not much left.

A few days later the soldiers came to arrest all the young men. Four of them took responsibility for what had happened: my father, Stands Different, Howling Wolf, Ax Handle, and Yellow Cook. They tried them in Miles City and took them to prison, keeping them in a dark place and giving them bread and water. Ax Handle died in prison, and the other three came home weak and scrawny. My father and Yellow Cook died soon afterward, but Howling Wolf must have been tough, because he lived a long time.

Another tragic incident was the murder of Hugh Boyle, the nephew of a rancher, resulting in the execution of the two warriors who killed him.

One evening in September 1890 Hugh Boyle left the ranch of his uncle, Patrick Lynch, in search of stock. When he failed to return that evening, he was reported missing.

Three days later Boyle's body was discovered with two gunshot wounds, one in the chest and one in the head. Two young Cheyennes, Head Chief and Young Mule, were sought for the killing. It seems that Boyle had come upon the two Cheyennes in the act of butchering a freshly killed beef. Boyle objected, and Head Chief shot him.

Hoping to avoid further conflict, the Cheyennes made an offer of thirty horses for the dead man and were refused. The Cheyennes refused to surrender their young men who sent word through the Indian agent to the police that they would "die in your sight." (Orlan J. Svingen, *The Northern Cheyenne Indian Reservation*, 1877–1900, University Press of Colorado, pp. 85–86.)

The two young Cheyennes, preferring to die honorably in battle rather than be hanged, prepared themselves for war. They mounted their horses and charged the troops who had positioned themselves in a straight line like a firing squad. Head Chief was the first to fall, shot from his horse. Both young men were killed. They died like the young warriors they were.

Regardless of conflicts such as these, the early 1900s were relatively quiet years during which the reservation expanded and developed, and we adjusted to our new life.

The parents and grandparents continued to share their stories of the old days, but holding on to our traditional culture became increasingly difficult, as more and more we acquired the ways of the white man.

We learned how to raise cattle, becoming quite successful in doing so, increasing the original herd of 1000 cows and 40 bulls to 12,000 head by 1912.

We were less successful with farming and growing crops, because we still had major problems such as the short growing season, the alkaline soil, limited areas of tillable land in the narrow valleys between the mountains, and a small amount of rainfall.

In 1907 the BIA began helping us develop our first irrigation project, although here too there were problems, including flooding. Eventually we used a new type of farming called dry farming in which we planted mainly wheat that didn't require much water.

Despite the problems with farming, we experienced a growing sense of accomplishment due to our success with cattle raising. It helped us feel that we were becoming more self-sufficient.

Meanwhile, family members and relatives who commonly lived close together were successful in finding other ways to obtain food. People now planted gardens, harvested crops, and gathered roots and wild fruits. Others raised chickens or kept milk cows. Many women learned to can fruits, vegetables, and meats.

So increasingly, this was a good time. We were more and more able to support ourselves, and we lived in peace.

Off the reservation, Americans were beginning to get electricity, telephones, and automobiles. But we still continued to live the simple life of rural-farm America as in the late 1800s. If we wanted to travel any distance, we went by horse and wagon, and we traveled on the two dirt roads that crossed the reservation: a 60-mile trip took about three or four days; people would go in small groups and camp along the way. If friends from another area came to visit, they would usually stay overnight.

The large gatherings we used to have when we moved our camps to follow the game were a thing of the past. In these days of rationing, many people came together just to talk and share news. Gatherings were held in dance halls or tents for celebrations rather than in the open as before. Typically, these dance halls were round or octagonally shaped to better accommodate our tradition of dancing in a circle.

By 1910 many Cheyenne men had become good cowboys. They were expert

horsemen who worked well in caring for stock. This included rounding up cows and calves, branding the calves, marking their ears, vaccinating them, and castrating the bull calves.

Cowboys also worked as "lineriders," guiding lines of cattle from the reservation to the stockyards in Chicago and Omaha. Commonly, these cattle drives combined herds of several Cheyenne families. Cowboys were paid by the BIA for this work.

The elders call this early reservation period the Time of the Horse. Cheyennes loved their horses. They not only used them in working with stock but raced them and showed them off at celebrations and fairs each year.

At these events the Cheyennes competed against each other, and sometimes with the Crows, in horse, foot, and wagon races. The women showed off their own skills with produce, canned goods, and arts and crafts.

Christmas and the Fourth of July celebrations drew huge crowds of people from other tribes and other Cheyenne communities, and members of the local community gave away horses and goods to these visitors. These giveaways illustrated the value of generosity which was still considered important. The individuals and families who were able to make these giveaways, having been successful in raising horses or in other ways, received much honor for their generosity.

New growth

The seeds we planted in the early 1900s were sprouting. We still had conflicts with the US Government and Bureau of Indian Affairs about attempts to take away our culture and prevent us from running our own lives. But more and more there seemed to be new opportunities and possibilities.

We became US citizens. This was Congress' way of showing their appreciation for the many Indians who had volunteered to fight in World War I.

We became individual landowners: 1500 members of the tribe at that time were allotted 160 acres of land. However, the allotments weren't always fair and contributed to divisions within the tribe.

We individually owned cattle for the first time, rather than having it as part of the tribal herd. Yet, the Bureau decided who could sell or butcher his own cattle.

We saw the first steps taken to improve medical care. A hospital was built by the Bureau, and a nurse-dietician team was established on the reservation.

A few of our elders today remember those times or heard stories from their parents and grandparents.

Dorothy Flatness:

I grew up on the reservation with four sisters and a brother. We lived with my mom and dad in a big log house with three bedrooms, a kitchen, a living room, and a dining room.

My dad raised cattle and hired people to trail them to Colstrip, Montana, where they would load them on boxcars to take to market. He also owned race horses. Racing was very popular in those days, although today many boys don't ride or even try to own horses.

My dad helped a lot of his nieces and nephews get started in life, letting them stay at the house and teaching them things. This was common practice in those days. When times were hard, someone would pitch in and help out. We were one big family.

The school on the reservation was a one-room log house. We had one teacher, and all the children up to eighth grade were in that room, about 30 or 40 of them. I played basketball, and later when I went to the new school at the St. Labre Mission where the grades were separated, I played baseball and participated in track, relays, broad jumping and shot putting. We sometimes had competitions with other schools.

I also did beading and helped my mother with chores around the house. I dug for roots and picked cherries and chokeberries. Then I helped my mother make jelly out of them. We would also can or dry them, and we used chokeberries to make a pudding. We never bought any of our food or clothing because we didn't have any money, and we made these things ourselves. When I had free time I went horseback riding.

I was at the mission school only one year when I got tuberculosis and went to stay at the new Galen Sanitorium for 4 years. I was the first Indian there and they called me Princess. I was 20 when I got out.

I was married at 23 and had 5 children.

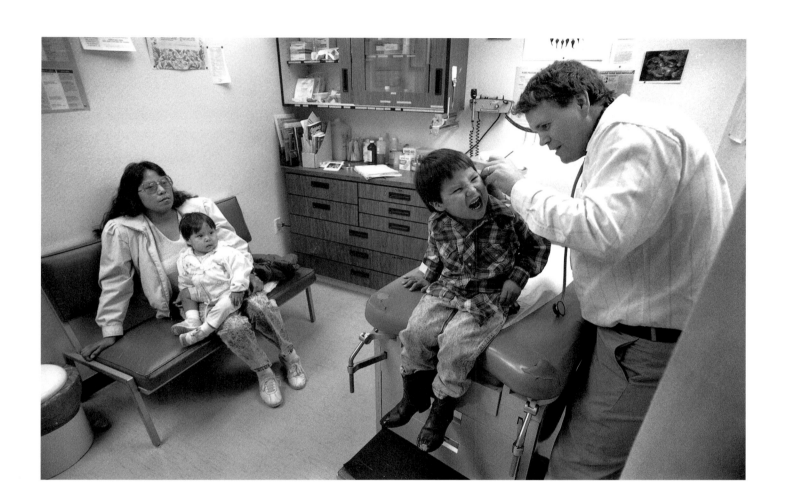

Helen Hiwalker:

I used to ride a Shetland pony to school. We had truant officers back then so we didn't dare miss school. They came on horseback and looked for you.

When I was in the sixth grade in the early 1930s, I got tuberculosis. They sent me to a girls and boys sanitorium that was run by the Bureau of Indian Affairs. I missed a year of school. They didn't have modern medicine then, but I recovered.

I finished the eighth grade at 14 and went to work baby-sitting for a woman who had three children. Besides baby-sitting, I cooked for everyone living there and also did the laundry. They paid me $7 a month for doing this. I went home on weekends.

I got married at 17, had my first child, and raised 8 children. Times were hard since my husband and I made only $20 a day. But the children's grandparents, Floyd and Belle Hiwalker, had cattle and they helped out.

My husband was a trick roper and rider and went to a lot of rodeos. Most of these were in Montana, but a few times he worked at Madison Square Garden.

I made extra money making buckskin shirts. I hand-tanned my own hides, then I decorated them with beads. It took 4 months to make a jacket, starting with soaking the buckskin to get the hair off of it, and then doing all of the stitching and beadwork. We used sinew from deer, elk, and cattle to sew with, since we didn't have nylon thread in those days. Later I used a pedal machine to sew on.

Rose Medicine Elk is the last member of the Quill Society, a women's group that practiced the ancient art of quillwork.

My parents asked old lady Dives Backwards to take and teach me the proper way to do quillwork. They took gifts to her—blankets, coffee, tobacco—and she accepted me. To begin my training, I had to go live with the old lady for a long time.

The Quill Society has died out. I'm the only one left. Very few people know how to do quillwork, or if they do, don't do it in the traditional way. Not like the way we were taught.

Rose Medicine Elk sharing her beading knowledge.

The Great Depression of the 1930s that impacted the rest of the country also hit us hard. To alleviate the unemployment, the BIA set up five Civilian Conservation Corp (CCC) camps on the reservation. The men who worked in these camps put up and repaired fences, developed springs, built reservoirs, constructed lookout towers, created trails for trucks, and fought fires and insects. It was a time of high employment.

When the Depression was over the CCC program ended, and the Cheyennes were without jobs. To add to the problem, many Cheyennes, during their participation in the

Victory Dance led by newly elected Senator Ben Nighthorse Campbell.

program, had leased their land to white ranchers. Now their only source of income was rent from the leases or welfare benefits. Poverty increased, and many turned to drinking.

On the positive side, the '30s marked a revival in our ability to govern ourselves again. In 1934 Congress passed the Indian Reorganization Act. Among other provisions, the Act created a loan program we could draw upon for the development of the reservation, permitted us to perform the Sun Dance again, and stopped the allotment of reservation lands so that we could once more own lands as a tribe. It also allowed us to form a tribal government.

Our people agreed to a new constitution which established the election of a tribal council and president, voting laws, and voting districts.

The Council took charge of tribal affairs, acting as business manager with the power to make contracts and agreements with outside organizations and agencies, distribute funds, and act as official spokesperson for the tribe. Although the Secretary of the Interior still had to approve any resolutions by the Council, we now had a voice to speak for us as one body.

Renewal

More and more, we were being drawn into the world.

During World War II, roughly 82 Cheyenne men and 4 women joined a branch of the armed forces. Many others worked off the reservation in war plants.

In the mid-1950s a new paved highway crossed our reservation, and we began to use cars and other modern devices. America was stirring, and we were stirring, too.

Many of our people began to shop in the larger towns outside the reservation. Horses were still important, but cars were what linked us to the larger world, along with the telephone and radio. These new inventions also brought the larger world to us, altering our culture in a number of

James King symbolizes the pride and patriotism of the Cheyenne people.

ways: for one, intermarriage between Cheyennes and whites became customary, resulting in the eventual deterioration of our language.

When the Cheyenne veterans returned home from World War II, we treated them as heroes, celebrating their return with victory dances and giveaways. This was also true following the Korean War in the 1950s in which many Cheyennes served. And later, in the '60s, 145 Cheyennes went to Vietnam.

The American flag, along with the Morning Star flag, is proudly raised in the Cheyenne camp of the Sacred Arrow ceremony in honor of the Cheyenne veterans who fought and laid down their lives so that we might have the freedom to worship in the way our Creator instructed us, and in this way continue the way of life given to the Cheyenne people.

Rubie Sooktis expresses the Cheyenne viewpoint on serving in the military for a country that had taken away Indian sovereignty:

There's a tremendous respect for the men and women who serve in the American wars, from World War I to Desert Storm. The returning veterans have a very significant role in our society; I think we depend on them. They replace the old warriors who, in the Sun Dance ceremony, told us their war deeds. So they are a very critical part of the Cheyenne world. I think the larger society needs to learn from that, from what we feel in our hearts about our country and about our flag that we adopted.

The stories our soldiers brought back with them about how Americans and Europeans lived in their cities made us aware that we needed to improve our own living conditions on the reservation, including finding more jobs for people. Some of the veterans helped in this effort by serving on the Tribal Council to work on making things better for our people.

For many Cheyenne veterans, however, the road to independence was a long, hard one. Windy Shoulderblade served in Vietnam and tells about his return to civilian life.

In Vietnam there were so many things we were trained to do. This was the one time in many of our lives when we were respected, we were needed, and we felt a part of something. Then, all of a sudden, within a few days time, you come back out of the jungle, are flown from Vietnam to the states, and then you're back on the reservation.

It was hard to find a job. I remember applying for jobs and not being hired, and consequently, there was a struggle . . . drinking a lot more; I became an alcoholic. That was my life. And my decision at that time was to die drinking, because I felt there was no reason to live. We didn't understand at the time that it was part of a post-traumatic stress disorder about feeling guilty about being alive when so many guys were killed in Vietnam. It was hard to break away from that frame of mind, and after a period of time you felt, why go on living?

After three or four years of that I finally decided that maybe there was something to live for. With the help of a minister who rescued me at the lowest point in my life, taking me home and caring for me, I learned that I was somebody, that I was valuable, a precious human being. That was the turning point for me.

Windy Shoulderblade entered tribal politics and became tribal president. But his struggle with alcohol wasn't over. After 12 years of sobriety, he suffered another setback. This time he entered the Veterans Center in Billings, Montana, where he confronted his problems, finally getting on top of them. He went on to become a minister, touring the reservations and ministering to inmates at local and state prisons. He became an important member of the college board during its critical building period, and he presently serves on the board of the Dull Knife Memorial Foundation.

Opportunities

Although unemployment remained high on the reservation during the '60s and '70s, job opportunities began to open up.

Many Indian workers were hired by Guild Arts and Crafts, an Eastern firm that relocated near the reservation and specialized in plastic novelties to be used by organizations in fundraising, and in costume jewelry. Its success in this venture led the Guild to increase its production. As a result, the Tribal Council invested $100,000 to construct a new plant which it leased to the company for this expanded production.

Other sources of employment opened up through the BIA, the school system including the St. Labre Indian School, and the tribe itself. The US Forest Service hired the younger men for fire fighting. Additional employment was provided by various federal programs and a few private enterprises both on and off the reservation.

Interior of the chapel at St. Labre Indian School.

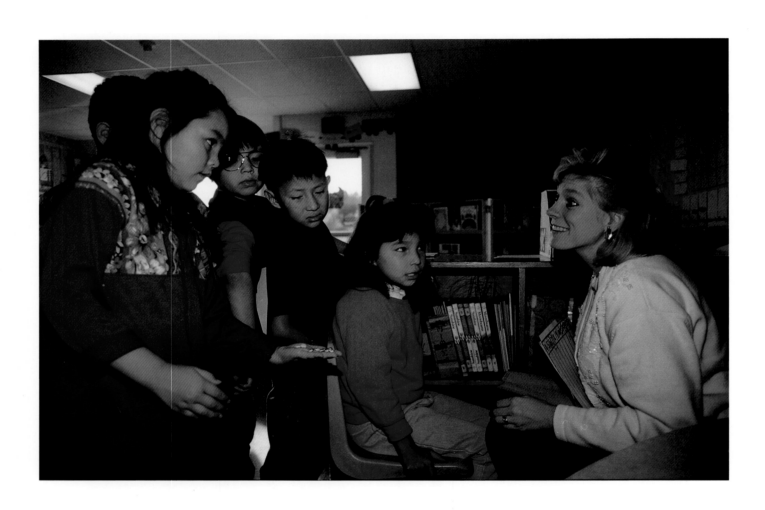

All of these developments helped raise living standards for the people who now had the opportunity to use their increased income for new products such as cars and telephones.

Discovering new strengths

By the 1970s we felt strong again. Not only were we finding new economic opportunities through our growing cattle herds, coal mining operations, and small business developments but our Tribal Council, rather than the Bureau, was making the decisions for us.

A dispute over mineral rights led to a Supreme Court decision granting the tribe mineral rights on our own land in perpetuity. This resulted in the tribe having control over the prospective development of mining operations on the reservation.

Education of our children in the basic elementary American curricula had begun as early as our confinement in Oklahoma and continued with the boarding schools in the early reservation years. Improved education in the '70s began with the Head Start program for preschoolers and expanded with the use of modern teaching techniques such as team teaching and the use of Cheyenne teacher aides.

A Teachers Workshop was created by the leadership of the Tribal Council to introduce teachers (most of whom were non-Indian) to programs and techniques for instructing Indian children; and to provide them with information about our way of life, history, and culture. In turn, the schools themselves began offering courses on our history.

As a result, our children began to show more interest in learning than ever, and this inspired parents to take part in the education of their children. As Cheyenne parents and elders became more involved in the education process, some began speaking in schools about our culture and values, while others taught courses in arts and crafts. Still others served on the now Indian-controlled school boards.

Ted Risingsun reminds us of the prophetic words of Chief Dull Knife:

One of the things that Chief Dull Knife said repeatedly was that we can no longer live the way we are living. We are going to learn a new way of life. Let's ask for schools so that our children can go to these schools and learn this new way of life.

Many had not the vision of Chief Dull Knife and opposed him. But in time, our people realized the wisdom of his words and from then on never turned their backs on the mission to improve the education of our children.

This mission culminated in the establishment of the Dull Knife Memorial College in 1975.

Dull Knife Memorial College
The beginnings

We feel our children need education which gives the best of both cultures. We feel that many of the values of our past Cheyenne society can still serve as well in this modern world. We feel we need this to give us understanding and pride in our past, just as other Americans learn their history for the same reason.

Education is important to our people. We conceive education not only in terms of classroom teaching, but as a process which begins at birth and continues throughout a life span.

Dull Knife Memorial College is a vital part of the Cheyenne people. Educating our young people is not pointed in the direction of a return to the past; neither is it designed to remove Indian people from retaining identification with their particular heritage. It opens the possibilities for Indian people to play an active role in evolving modes of life they consider important for being a Cheyenne in the world of today and tomorrow.

As a people we have met challenges before. The spiritual energy of the Cheyenne brought them back to our homeland. Every generation must have the strength to fight for survival. Sweet Medicine, the prophet, told the people, We must not forget who we are.

Through education, the young people can observe and learn. They will be our leaders one day.

The young people are the essence of life.

John Woodenlegs
Former Tribal Council president

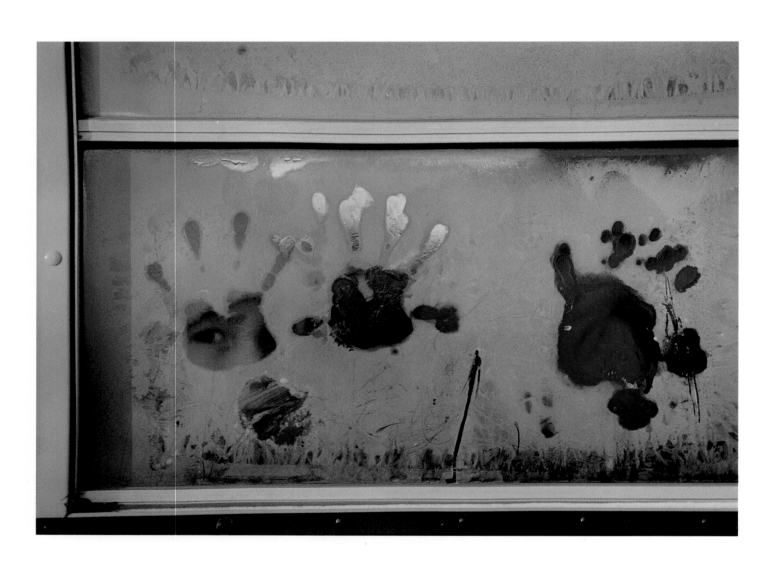

The predecessor of the College was a program called the Northern Cheyenne Resource Development, Inc., a corporation providing vocational training for jobs in the building of nearby coal-firing generating plants and in mining operations. The training was held at the St. Labre Indian School in the old monastery and church and included vocational trades such as heavy equipment operators, welders, carpenters, and engineers.

In September 1975 the Northern Cheyenne Tribal Council chartered the school under the name of the Northern Cheyenne Indian Action Program and moved it to Lame Deer.

Soon after, members of the Board of Directors of the Northern Cheyenne Indian Action Program asked themselves: Where are we going? Do we want to get accredited as a vocational school? Do we want to be a college? We had been experimenting with and offering some academic classes, and they were very popular. And so we made a decision to become a college.

In 1977 the name was officially changed to Dull Knife Memorial College. Academic as well as vocational classes were offered.

The College began with a single facility at Lame Deer consisting of one large building with six classrooms, four shop areas, and three rooms for offices. Since 1978 the College has expanded to include additional classrooms and office space, a cafeteria, a large auditorium, and library.

Founding board members of the Northern Cheyenne Indian Action Program were:

Ted Risingsun

Doreen Pond

Llevando "Cowboy" Fisher

Joseph Bahr

Raymond Spang

Daniel Foote

In 1979 we began the process of becoming accredited as a 2-year community college. Previously, Indians desiring an education beyond high school had to travel 100 miles to attend college. Now they could receive this education on the reservation.

Becoming fully accredited was a 6-year process. Unfortunately, in 1986 the College was denied accreditation, largely due to financial difficulties. We were advised to close the doors for two years, reorganize, rename, and try again.

Father Emmett supports the dream of education for Cheyenne children of all ages.

Not willing to give up the dream of providing higher education for our children, the Board chose to keep the College operating, in spite of what appeared to be overwhelming odds.

Coauthor Doreen Pond has been involved with the College since its beginnings. She recalls those difficult times.

The struggle to keep the College open was not unlike the struggle of our ancestors to reach Montana from Oklahoma. The odds seemed insurmountable. When Art McDonald came on as president in 1986, the College was carrying a debt of nearly $900,000. For the next eight years we were worried that we wouldn't have enough money to open or continue operating for the school year.

But we had a board that believed in the important mission of the College to educate our people, and that belief alone helped us continue from year to year.

We had to reduce the staff, an extremely difficult decision. And we worked on getting three other accredited schools to accept our credits for student transfers, even though we were no longer a candidate for accreditation ourselves. And with this accomplished, we were able to go to Washington and ask that our funding be restored so we could open our doors.

At last we got the financial help we needed. Father Emmett Hoffmann of the St. Labre Indian School believed in our dream and wanted to help, but first he needed a commitment from the two of us that we would remain with the College, see it through its difficulties. Art and I agreed. Satisfied that we would stay the course, St. Labre gave us $200,000 toward our $900,000 debt.

Fr. Hoffmann also taught me the techniques of fundraising, saying, "The only thing you can do is learn to help yourself." Eight years later we had turned the donations we received, and which we saved, into the $1 million endowment we have today.

In 1988 the College was again accepted as a candidate in the accreditation process; and in June 1996, the process completed, Dull Knife Memorial College received accreditation.

During the time Dull Knife Memorial College was struggling to hang on, the entire

educational system on the Northern Cheyenne Reservation was at risk. Norma Bixby, Tribal Education Director and chairperson of the College Board of Directors, explains why.

In 1982, I was hired as the career development director of a program which provided scholarships for higher education and adult vocational training. I found that students were not ready to attend college. Our scholarship program had a high drop-out rate. The retention rate was about 50 percent, and we had only one or two graduates a year. I knew then that a coordinated effort involving all the schools was needed to improve education.

Our high school students were going on to any one of five schools on or near the reservation, even though the college was here. Students often transferred back and forth between schools, they were dropping out, and there were many discipline problems. Basically they were not getting a good education.

Through the need to improve education for Northern Cheyenne children and the need to coordinate efforts, the Northern Cheyenne Tribal Education Commission was established. As its new director, I put much of my focus into working to establish a new high school for the reservation. I felt we needed a complete educational system from Head Start to college. The local public school systems felt we did not need a high school and objected strongly to its development. But we didn't give up, and the new high school opened its doors for the first time in the 1994-95 school year.

Having a complete educational system has helped Dull Knife Memorial College to grow. High school students can now transfer from a high school on the reservation right into college. In addition, the College can assist those students who have poor academic backgrounds to be better prepared to enter college and to graduate.

That the College was worth saving is measured by its successes.
Doreen Pond:

I have had some people come in and talk to me, saying, "I don't have the skills to make it." They are hesitant to try, because they have been beaten down so much in life, they don't want to expose themselves again to failure. Then they can say, "Well, I never really tried," and it allows them to maintain that little thread of self-respect. To see students like that develop the self-esteem necessary to achieve their goals, become leaders in the community, and advocates for the children, is rewarding.

Helping students overcome obstacles to education is an important goal of the College. Paula Woodenlegs, graduate, tells how the assistance she received at a difficult time in her life contributed to her success.

I am half Cheyenne and Chippewa Cree and I grew up on the reservation. After I finished the eighth grade at the Lame Deer school and graduated from St. Labre Mission School, I went on to Miles City Community College. But I got sick and had to return home. Then I attended a college in Northern Montana where my mother had gone, but I didn't fit in.

After one year of nursing I returned to the reservation and entered Dull Knife Memorial College. In the meantime I'd married, and just as I was ready to graduate I became pregnant with my son. There were difficulties in the delivery, and I was paralyzed. I had to learn to walk again. And I didn't have any money for school, and neither my husband nor I had a job.

Then one of the teachers at the College urged me to come back, saying, "You're one class away from graduation," and he said the school could help me. That's when I met Doreen Pond and she put me in the Co-op Program where I worked for credit plus a small wage.

That helped my family, and I was able to graduate in 1989. Soon after that I began work at the College as a clerk and worked my way up to become an administrative assistant. Recently I started doing public relations work. This has been a real breakthrough for me. It's helped my self-esteem....

The graduates of the class of 1990 reflect the achievements of students at Dull Knife Memorial College. Many have gone on to higher learning. Others have found meaningful employment.

Lydia Burke. Union Services Representative in Colstrip, MT.

Barbara Clubfoote. B.S. in Human Services from Salish Kootenai College. Currently employed with the Northern Cheyenne tribal court system.

Lorna Elliott. Currently employed at a resort area in White Sulphur Springs, MT.

Clarence Kaline. Teacher with the Ashland Head Start Program.

Austin Two Moons and Father Emmett asking Maheo for peace.

Ruth Castillo, proud Dull Knife graduate.

Myron Littlebird. Consultant to the Northern Cheyenne Recovery Center.

Karla McDonald. B.S. in Alcohol and Drug Studies from the University of South Dakota; M.A. in Counseling from the University of Montana. Currently Substance Abuse Counselor for Indian Health Service in Crow Agency, MT.

Diana Means. B.S. in Nursing from Montana State University. Currently on leave from Indian Health Service to pursue advanced nurses training in Boston, MA.

Quentin Means. Currently employed with Northern Cheyenne Ambulance Service.

Curtis One Bear. Studying architecture at Montana State University.

Patricia Aragon Peppers. B.S. in Computer Science from Eastern Montana College. Currently Data Management Specialist at Dull Knife Memorial College.

Leslie Spang. Custodian for Dull Knife Memorial College.

Susanne Starr. Currently employed with Indian Health Service in the Community Health Nursing Program.

Christine Valentine. Private consultant to the Northern Cheyenne Recovery Center.

At the present time the drop-out rate at Dull Knife Memorial College is 15 percent, way below the national average of 85 percent for Indian students at other colleges.

The mission statement and objectives of the College have gone through several revisions since the school's inception and now read as follows:

Mission Statement

Dull Knife Memorial College is an open-admission, community-based, comprehensive, tribally controlled community college and land grant institution designed to provide afford-able, quality educational opportunities to residents of the Northern Cheyenne Reservation and surrounding communities. The College is named in honor of one of the Northern Cheyenne's most respected historical leaders who fought overwhelming odds to maintain the sovereignty of the Cheyenne people, a century before the College's first academic courses were offered in 1978. Reflecting Chief Dull Knife's determination, the College's primary mission is to provide educational and cultural leadership to its constituents.

Dull Knife Memorial College operates on the belief that all individuals should be:

Treated with dignity and respect.

Afforded equal opportunity to acquire a complete educational experience.

Given an opportunity to discover and develop their special aptitudes and insights.

Provided an opportunity to equip themselves for a fulfilling life and responsible citizenship in a world characterized by change, while simultaneously studying and enhancing Cheyenne cultural values.

Goals

The following goals have been adopted by the Dull Knife Memorial College Board of Directors. Originally stated in 1979 as purposes of the College by the Board of Directors and Tribal Council, the goals were modified in 1982, 1987, and 1992, as part of the College's long-range planning efforts.

Dull Knife Memorial College seeks:

To be financially stable and self-sufficient.

To provide educational resources and experiences to assist community members in acquiring improved skills for work and life.

To achieve an accredited institution of higher education on the Northern Cheyenne Reservation capable of providing college transfer programs and vocational training necessary to increase the educational level and meet the training needs of students and community.

To enhance educational opportunities and provide a research program to preserve, teach, and support traditional Cheyenne culture, language, and history.

Having made a major start, and seeing our dreams for a college come true, we needed to do more: ensure its survival. To do this, in 1992 we took the next step and created the Dull Knife Memorial Foundation.

The moon rises over the fire
The coyotes howl at the beauty of the water
And the moon itself.
As the snow sparkles in the moonlight
The ice glimmers
The fire glows in front of the tepee
And the Indian culture lives on.

O nce, in the fall of our days, the buffalo was central to our lives. It provided us with food, clothing, shelter, all the necessities of life.

In the winter of our lives, the buffalo, taken from us, reappeared as the Bureau of Indian Affairs that became the sustenance upon which we depended for our existence.

Now it is summer, and once more we are strong. We have the Foundation. This is our buffalo now.

Summer is a time when the seeds of the year planted in the spring begin to come into full bloom. It is a time when the warmth of the sun is strong and healing.

And so it was for us. We had gone through many hard times when the roots of our traditional culture were cut. But they were not entirely severed, and summer offered us a chance for regeneration and renewal.

In the early summer, things were still difficult for us, but we could see progress. More and more, we were gaining control over our lives. Our economy was improving, and we were becoming more self-sufficient.

The birth of our college brought even more possibilities as our people learned about our traditions and the skills they needed to compete in the world. With a foundation in place, we would have a vehicle for raising funds and helping our people economically.

As late summer approaches, it is time to look to the future, to new prospects for growth, so that we can harvest even greater opportunities when fall comes around again.

And the journey of life will be complete once more as we begin anew.

The Foundation

We didn't start out talking about a foundation. Initially we were thinking about ways to make the Dull Knife Memorial College self-sufficient. And then we realized we not only needed to create a financial future for the College but for our people generally.

An important guiding ideal was to be independent of government subsidies and influence. And we wanted to protect the abilities of our visionaries who had many ideas to help our people; and we wished to share this knowledge with others.

Coauthor Art McDonald explains why the creation of a foundation was of paramount importance.

Dennis Limberhand completing his leg of a commemorative run from Bear Butte to Lame Deer.

Even with the endowment, the College was under continuous financial pressure. With BIA funding threatened every year, we needed to make the College less dependent on this source. So we brought the school up to where it owes nothing and now operates within budget.

But we wanted more than that, because there aren't any new moneys in the BIA, and we've stabilized in the number of students we're going to serve. So while we can budget from year to year, the future is critical. This was brought home to us very clearly this year by the failure of Congress and the federal government to even provide us with a budget.

Rubie Sooktis, board member, expresses her concerns.

I wanted a long-term financial life for the College. There are a lot of beautiful ideas here on the reservation, but they only go as far as the funding goes. For one thing, we want to be able to offer the excellent teachers we have here continuous work; and we want to provide free education to our people.

And so the Dull Knife Memorial Foundation was born, and it took a team to do that. It took the administration, it took Doreen, it took Art, it took the Board, and it took the belief that we were going to come together and accomplish something.

The Foundation was established to protect the assets of our people, to protect our culture, and to perpetuate our language. These were our initial goals which grew into an expanded vision of the future, one that would offer hope and a chance for a better life for all of our people.

Bill Tallbull's' prayer of a Vision of Hope given at the dedication of the Museum and Visitors Center at Fort Phil Kearny, in honor of those who had fought and died there in 1866, expresses the sentiments of all who have worked hard to create a vision for the Foundation. Included in the prayer were these words:

I beg the Sacred Grandfathers to give us their special blessings so that our Creator will give us a new dawn of hope, and that the goodness of life will be our constant companion in our pursuit of justice, happiness, and freedom for all Americans.

Ben Nighthorse Campbell greets a relative, Mary Fisher, Cheyenne elder.

Philosophy of the Foundation

We created the Dull Knife Memorial Foundation in 1992 in memory of Chief Dull Knife's trek from Fort Robinson, Nebraska Territory, to our home in Montana, inasmuch as the Foundation is similarly designed to aid our people in their continued trek toward excellence.

The Foundation supports our College, and with many other projects helps our people as well. Our hope is to bring the traditional wisdom of the Cheyenne people to the struggling world, even as we bring the technology of this world to our people.

The Foundation is a state-chartered, nonprofit 501(c)(3) mutual benefit corporation which is organized exclusively for charitable, educational, and scientific purposes, and for providing services to the community. As expressed in our statement of purposes and goals, these include:

Increasing public awareness of Native American heritage.

Supporting education and research including presentations by means of exhibits, symposia, publications, and other educational programs.

Conducting or supporting programs for Dull Knife Memorial College.

Making distributions to historical societies, preservation organizations, museums, colleges and universities, and other organizations that qualify as exempt organizations under Section 501(c)(3).

Developing economic and business projects to provide job and housing opportunities to the Northern Cheyenne tribal members.

In short, the Foundation serves as our guide as we work to improve the present and plan for the future. As John Woodenlegs, tribal elder, expressed it:

As the Morning Star has been
our guiding light
So it will give us life in our hearts
and will guide us
in the days to come.

These are the Foundation's present board members:

Norma Bixby

Tony Foote

Emmett Hoffmann

T.R. Hughes

Art McDonald

Doreen Pond

Windy Shoulderblade

Rubie Sooktis

Our vision of the Foundation

We feel it's important not only to identify and preserve but to celebrate the survival values of our tribe, those skills that have been developed over the years of our struggles and have brought us to this place in history. We understand that these values are not universal but connected to a particular place; that the knowledge one needs to survive are different from one community to another; and that schools, both public and private, ought to teach the survival skills appropriate for that community.

Further, we do not believe any society can survive without a sense of community, without that sense of identity or roots that we call tribalism, that tells us who we are. Perhaps many Americans feel lost and rootless because they have lost their sense of community and identity.

In turn, we do not believe any society can sustain itself unless it reveres the wisdom of its elders. They are the ones who know what the values of a community are and how to communicate them to the younger generation. This is one of the gifts we want to share with others who have lost that vision.

For we believe there is a circle of life that gives purpose to all humanity, and the elders are part of this circle. With age comes wisdom, and that wisdom can be passed on to the young. Thus, the circle is complete.

This is true not only for our own society, but for any tribe, family, school, city, or nation.

J enny Medicine Woman Morrisson

The tradition of flute making is passed on to J.D. Old Mouse.

Our hopes for the future

The Foundation's goal is to continue the dream of Chiefs Dull Knife and Little Wolf, as it's been carried on by their direct descendants—Ted Risingsun, great-grandson of Chief Dull Knife, and Bill Tallbull, great-grandson of Chief Little Wolf.

A century ago, Chief Dull Knife foresaw education as a way to increase opportunities for the Cheyenne people. He also believed that our wisdom, culture, and way of life were not just for the tribe but for all humanity.

Bill Tallbull, in speaking to his students at Dull Knife Memorial College, gave them this rock to stand on:

We seem to be lost in this society. People don't even know what the problem is, or what a family is to do. When you're lost, you try to find things familiar to you. Let's, for a moment, take ourselves to the north of the Platte River in Wyoming. The river is in front of us, it's familiar, and we're just standing there. But if we stand somewhere else that is strange to us, we have a feeling that we're lost.

The thing about the river that is familiar is that the Cheyenne have lived up and down this river. They hunted in this river, they established a relationship with the river itself and with everything around it. When you think about that relationship, you're no longer lost. You know where you are, and you become part of that.

You can say, "I am the descendant of so-and-so who used to come up and down this river and who established a relationship with it. Here I am." All of a sudden you're not lost. You're part of something that has been established a long time ago.

Our dreams for the future

We have bold dreams for the Foundation's future, dreams that might seem daunting had we not already overcome impossible odds to get where we are today. So we go forward with faith in our ability to change and adapt as circumstances demand.

The symbolic figure of Christ as a Cheyenne sundancer decorated by Chief James D. Little Coyote for the St. Labre Chapel.

Below are some of those dreams.

Assisting the elderly. It is crucial that the Foundation be concerned with taking care of our elderly people. They are the "walking libraries of the past," and it is important to keep them among us to share their traditions. Therefore, it is essential that we develop **assisted living facilities** in every community that can economically maintain such a unit. In that way we would be honoring our elders, as is our traditional way.

Scholarship program. It is important for the Foundation to develop an **endowment fund** for scholarships for Indian students, regardless of where or what discipline they choose to study. It is vital to the Indian way of life to educate the young, not only for the development of the individual but for whatever service these scholars can give back to the community. This includes scholarship money for students that graduate from Dull Knife Memorial College and go on to higher learning.

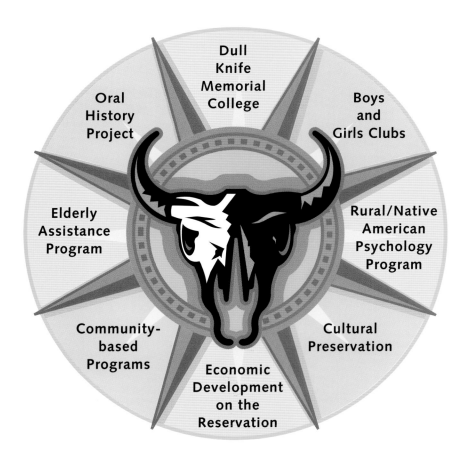

College support. It is critical to the Foundation's mission to raise funds that will **guarantee the future of Dull Knife Memorial College.** That's what we initially set out to do, and this effort will continue to be a primary priority. The peculiarities of tribal college funding basically preclude the building of facilities on the funding provided by Congress. Therefore, in order to provide students with a well-rounded educational experience, it is necessary for the Foundation to find the funds for building programs that include libraries and student activity centers at tribal colleges. The Foundation is committed to offering this support wherever possible.

Community projects. An important component of our dream is to join with other institutions on the reservation in cooperative efforts to provide service to the community, particularly as it applies to training inhabitants in those kinds of behaviors that are conducive to self-determination. One such example is the Boys & Girls Clubs of America: a chapter was initiated and maintained by community members on the Northern Cheyenne Reservation with no outside promotion. The Club has been very successful and serves as a highlight of community development for the entire reservation.

The Foundation has supported this project by providing funds for a Feeding Program for Needy Youth, which provides meals or emergency food for youth club members. It is the hope of the Foundation that we can generate enough funds to be a **resource for organizations** such as this one.

Preserving our culture. Part of the dream of the Foundation is to be able to issue grants to individuals and/or institutions in order that they might conduct activities that will enhance the **preservation of Cheyenne culture.** Typically, most community colleges are not charged with archival or historical preservation duties. However, tribal colleges are the only institutions in existence that have the responsibility for the maintenance and preservation of their particular tribal history, culture, and traditions.

Since the funding of tribal colleges is restricted exclusively to the number of students taught, there is no provision for moneys to be allocated for the preservation of tribal culture. Thus, it is extremely important that the Foundation raise the funds to provide for this function.

Psychological Services Program. Since, as mentioned above, the College does not receive funds to provide services beyond the teaching of students, the Foundation recognizes the importance of providing the resources so that our academic institution may offer a variety of **mental health services** as is necessary in support of the students, including mental health training. It should be pointed out that psychological services include more than mental health service delivery; it becomes as well the vehicle through which any psychological research in the community is delivered. (See discussion below on how psychology was brought to the reservation.)

Research. Tribal colleges must take on many of the characteristics of a land grant institution in that each has to be the institution that provides the research and extension service to the reservation. Consequently, it is our dream to be able to raise the funds necessary to **initiate and maintain a tribal research component** much as is done with mainstream institutions with land grant status. It is crucial that future research conducted on the reservation be performed by inhabitants of the reservation, and that those inhabitants have the opportunity to learn how to conduct appropriate research, in order that advances can be made in identifying needs and applying solutions.

Economic development. The Foundation has a dream of being able to **initiate feasible businesses** and ways of making a living that is culturally relevant without causing dissonance within the parameters of the reservation or between its inhabitants. Accordingly, the economic development plans of the Foundation to meet the needs of the reservation's depressed economy will be to provide a role-model effect through demonstration projects such as developing small shops and providing management training at the academic institution. When training has progressed to the point that the trainee can successfully manage the business, the business will be sold to that person at cost. The money received from the sale will then be rolled over into the next business, and the process continues. It is our basic philosophy that small businesses run by individuals are key to the economic health of communities such as Indian reservations.

Language preservation. **Preservation and teaching of the Northern Cheyenne language** is the responsibility of the total community with the focus on Dull Knife Memorial College. Here again, there are no funds awarded the College for the development of this kind of activity; the Foundation must provide them. Rather than teaching academically oriented Cheyenne language courses, however, classes will be taught by our elders (who know the language far better than any certified teacher) in the traditional manner. A way must be developed to combine the Head Start and assisted-living components so that that the utilization of the elders in a dignified way as teachers can become a reality.

Bringing psychology to the reservation

Art McDonald, the second American Indian to receive a Ph.D. in Psychology, worked to bring the benefits of psychology to the reservation.

He perceived that the problems usually associated with reservations such as low self-image, alcoholism, high unemployment, high accident rates, violence, etc., were not problems unique to the reservation. It was his impression that issues involved with economics—extreme poverty, overcrowding, related crime, lack of hope—were problems visible in all the cities and countries he visited.

The major noticeable difference, however, was the approach to dealing with these problems. The cities seemed to have a wide variety of resources, many of which were either attributed to, controlled by, or elements of the academic institutions. What was apparent was that the rural communities simply did not have those resources nor the accompanying academic institutions, and the sovereign Indian reservations especially were void of these kinds of services.

Although numerous attempts have been initiated by major academic institutions to provide outreach into the rural community, these have not been successful primarily because a) they are meeting the needs of the institution rather than the community; and b) classes are typically transposed from the academic institutions to the rural community. The more appropriate and successful efforts have been the tribal colleges.

Once the Dull Knife Memorial College was established, the base for providing parallel mental health services using the academic institution as its vehicle became possible. Assistantships were then provided to graduate students from APA-approved (American Psychological Association) programs during which the students came to the reservation and provided services in counseling, school psychology, consulting, and research.

Hilda and Austin Two Moons. His grandfather, Two Moon, fought in the Battle of Little Bighorn.

At the same time, the student received much-needed instruction from the local community. This came about with courses taught by Bill Tallbull: *The Foundations of the Oral Tradition, Ethnobotany,* and *Approaches to Healing.* The elders of the community were brought in to teach these mental health graduate students some of the important philosophy toward healing as it has been developed and passed on through many, many generations. This arrangement was reciprocal: the local community received professional level services by individuals that were not available through any other medium; and future psychologists were exposed to the needs of the reservation world, learning in the process to be more sensitive to diversity issues, regardless of where they might go to teach and practice.

Art McDonald believes that one of the most important lessons the Cheyenne people can teach future academic psychologists revolves around a philosophy based on the tribal worldview which is holistic and complete. It does not lend itself to discussion or scientific analysis. Thus, there is a conflict between the tribal worldview and modern humanistic psychology, the latter of which stresses the ideal of self-actualization, that is, encouraging the individual to develop his or her potential to the fullest.

Although personal achievement is admirable, it is counterproductive unless it includes the larger organizational structure — family, tribe, society. The Indian point of view is that survival of the group is the important goal and takes precedence over the values and behaviors of the self-indulging individual.

The overriding approach to delivery of mental health services must be the empowerment of the individual functioning at his/her highest level in order for the community to remain strong and healthy. That way the entire community grows, and the individuals within also grow as part of the whole.

Such values are extremely important to all groups of individuals who have a sense of communal identity and think of themselves in and belonging to a particular place. This is true without regard to race, gender, or religion. So whether you graduate from Lame Deer High School or from any high school in small-town America, that community owns you forever. Whether you do well or not, you will always remain a part of that community, and the community will rejoice with you if you reach your goals and feel badly for you if you do not.

As part of its mission, the Foundation has a goal of continuing to get more Native American students into the pipeline to become practicing psychologists as well as continuing its mission to provide quality professional mental health services at the reservation level.

Protecting the Earth

We created the Foundation to tell our story in a positive way and to help others so that together we can all protect the earth. Bill Tallbull said it best:

From the time the Indian first set foot upon the continent, he has centered his life on the natural world. He is deeply invested in the earth, committed to it both in conscience and in his instinct. In him the sense of place is paramount; only in reference to the earth can he persist in his true identity.

There is, on the part of most people in your society, a tacit assumption that the land is a commodity, an object of trade and utility. But for the Indian this is a false view, a failure to imagine the landscape truly, in our own terms. The landscape cannot be appropriated to individual ownership but rather is there for all men alike, as a dimension in which they have existence with other creatures.

For the Indian conceives of himself in terms of the land. Landscape is his natural element, it is the only dimension in which his life is possible. A notion that he is independent of the earth, that he can be severed from it and remain whole, does not occur to him; such a notion is false and would therefore be unworthy of him.

In his view the earth is sacred, it is a living entity in which entities have origin and destiny. The Indian does not lose sight of it ever; he is bound to the earth forever in his spirit. By means of his involvement in the natural world does the Indian ensure his own well-being. You see, I stand in good relation to the earth.

We have always had the example of deep, ethical regard for the land. We had better learn from it. Surely the ethic is nearly latent in ourselves. It must now be activated. We Americans must come again to the moral comprehension of the land and air. We must live according to the principle of a land ethic. The alternative is that we shall not live at all.

Ecology is perhaps the most important subject of our time. I cannot think of an issue in which the Indian has more authority or a greater stake. If there is one thing which truly distinguishes him, it is surely his regard of and for the natural world.

Being Cheyenne

We are proud to be Cheyenne. This is what it means to some of us, in our own words.

Windy Shoulderblade:

I look back to my grandfather, my father and my mother, to them being Cheyenne. Being an Indian was a person who, in spite of the pressures, was able to overcome difficulties and setbacks with the strength that comes from within. Not depending on their own strength but depending on a supernatural strength that comes from God, and being open to receive that strength. Being able to take time for prayer and meditation. And that is indicative of the Cheyennes throughout our history.

Paula Woodenlegs:

To me, being a Cheyenne is everything I've learned from my grandparents, from the community, and from the College. It's everything I've learned that has helped me go forward, to be proud of who I am and the things I've been taught, to be able to pass these values on to my children. That's what it is to be Cheyenne.

Doreen Pond:

I feel honored and privileged to have the family and community support that I've grown up with and to have had some of the knowledge of the elders passed down to me. I feel honored to have had my grandmother carry on the tradition of teaching us the stories and to have worked with John Woodenlegs, Ted Risingsun, and Bill Tallbull. They brought me along and believed in me. They were always willing to take the time to teach you. If you asked a question or if you were troubled, they were always there to lend support. Those three gentlemen are no longer with us. I will miss them tremendously.

John Woodenlegs always told us: "We're your family. Know who you are related to, where you come from. Even though you were raised in this family, your bloodline goes back to those in the past, those who died making their way back here. You were raised by them, too."

That's what it means to me to be Cheyenne.

John Woodenlegs also left us a beautiful legacy when he spelled out for us the values that we have tried to live by:

> Stay close to Spirit, our Creator. Pray for guidance and help.
>
> Respect one another as people.
>
> Be honest.
>
> Do what is right.
>
> Be gentle, kind, and peaceful.
>
> Help one another, each doing his share.
>
> Be good to one another, use no harsh words.
>
> Keep ourselves healthy and strong, in body and mind, because Spirit created us.
>
> Have reverence for the earth and all of life.
>
> Know how to take care of ourselves in the best way, learn to be responsible people, do our share of the responsibilities of living.
>
> Work for the good of all, not just ourselves.

Summer has indeed blossomed for us. We feel humble and grateful for all the good we have been privileged to receive. We look forward to the future with confidence and with the hope that we can share with all peoples those beliefs and values that have sustained us well.

> We are birds of many colors, red, blue, green, yellow.
> Yet it is all one bird.
> There are horses of many colors, brown, black, yellow, white.
> Yet it is all one horse, cattle, all living things.
> Animals, flowers, trees.
> So men in this land which once were only Indians are now many colors,
> White, black, yellow, red.
> All one people.
> That this should come to pass was in the heart of the Great Mystery.
> It is right thus, and
> Everywhere there shall be peace.
>
> Chief Highchief

The Authors

A rthur L. "Paints Many Horses" McDonald, Ph.D., is an enrolled member of the Oglala Sioux tribe. He is presently CEO of the Dull Knife Memorial Foundation of Lame Deer, Montana, and Director, Psychological Services/Institutional Research of the Dull Knife Memorial College. He is a member of the American Psychological Association. Dr. McDonald has coauthored numerous articles for publication in *Psychology Representative*, *Psychopharmacologia*, and *Journal of Psychology*, to name a few.

Dr. McDonald is also a recognized authority on the breeding and raising of performance quarter horses. His equine research has led to a developmental nutrition program for horses. He lives on a ranch with his wife Rita on the reservation in Lame Deer, Montana.

Doreen and daughter, Dr. Diane Pond at the 1993 Presidential Inauguration.

Doreen "Walking Woman" Pond is an enrolled member of the Northern Cheyenne tribe. She is Director of Development for the Dull Knife Memorial Foundation and a member of the Board. Ms. Pond received her B.A. in Administration and Community Development from Antioch College. She was the second woman to serve on the Cheyenne Tribal Council (serving three separate terms), the first being her grandmother. Involved with the Dull Knife Memorial College since its inception in 1973, Ms. Pond served as Dean of Business Affairs, Director of Institutional Development, and Vice President for Business Affairs. Her energies are now directed toward maintaining the viability of the Foundation.

Ms. Pond is married to Leland Pond, a practicing attorney and an enrolled member of the Assiniboin tribe. They reside on the Northern Cheyenne Reservation.

The McDonalds have three children and the Ponds, two. Four of the five have come through the reservation public school system. What is remarkable is the academic accomplishments of these young people, unusual for reservation children. It is the fervent hope of the Northern Cheyenne people that the success of these five will in the future become the norm for all reservation children. This is the mission of the College and the Foundation. Until that time, these young adults are an inspiration to all who come after them.

Forest R. McDonald received his education in Fine Arts at Spokane College. He is presently living in San Francisco where he continues his interest in the fine arts field.

Justin Douglas McDonald set the school record in shot put while in high school at Colstrip, Montana, continuing that success during his Navy tour of duty. He was an academic All-American while at the University of South Dakota where he earned his Ph.D. in Clinical Psychology. In 1992 Mr. McDonald was appointed Director of Indians in Psychology, a Congressionally funded program at the University of North Dakota.

Karla Marie McDonald graduated from Dull Knife Memorial College with a 2-year degree. She went on to the University of South Dakota to earn a B.S. in Alcohol and Drug Studies and an M.A. in Counseling from the University of Montana. In 1996 she accepted a position as Substance Abuse Counselor for the Indian Health Service at Crow Agency, Montana. Sharing her father's interest in horses, during the years 1978-1982 Ms. McDonald competed in the World Youth Quarter Horse Show.

Leland Pond Jr. has two bachelor of science degrees from the University of Montana, one in Medical Technology and another in Microbiology. He is currently pursuing a higher degree with an option to practice in the dental or medical field.

Diane Pond graduated with honors from Colstrip High School and went on to graduate with honors from the University of Montana. She was accepted at the Stanford Medical Center in California where she graduated, the first Northern Cheyenne woman to earn a doctor of medicine degree. Licensed to practice as an M.D., Ms. Pond is currently completing her residency at Stanford in Anesthesiology.

The authors with their families.

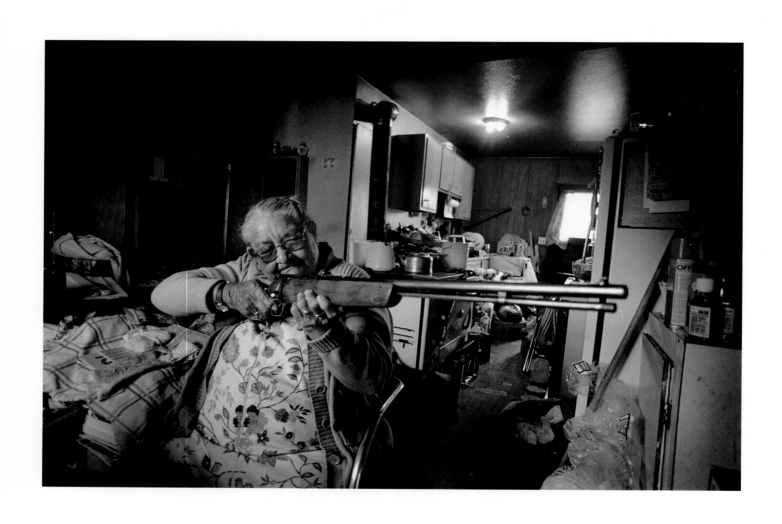

Thelma Two Two — proud, independent Cheyenne elder.

A bout the photographer . . .

John Warner has photographed life on the Northern Cheyenne Reservation in Montana since 1989.

Documenting the everyday life of the Northern Cheyenne people became a full-time job when he left his position as a staff photographer at the *Indianapolis Star* in 1991 and moved to the reservation to concentrate solely on this singular yet complex assignment. He is the staff photographer at the St. Labre Indian School.

It has been Warner's goal to create the most comprehensive photodocumentary of modern-day reservation life in recent history. The body of work selected for *Cheyenne Journey* speaks for itself.

Through the Foundation Father Emmett continues to bring hope and inspiration to today's youth.

Seven Locks Press publishes nonfiction work on contemporary issues and public affairs. For more information regarding our other publications or to order additional copies of *Cheyenne Journey*, please call 800-354-5348.